SPLIT SECOND CHOICE

The Power of Attitude

By James L. Winner
with George P. Thompson III

THE WINNERS • LOUISIANA

The Winners
2251 Drusilla Lane, Suite C
Baton Rouge, LA 70806
800-256-9222

First Edition

Printed and bound in the United States of
America.

Cover Graphic by Philip DeMahy
Edited by Mindy Averitt

Printed by Moran Printing, Inc.
Baton Rouge, Louisiana

Library of Congress Catalog Card Number 96-90824

ISBN 0-9655042-0-4

IN LOVING MEMORY

While I was growing up, I watched my parents constantly rise above the obstacles in their lives. They taught me that when you get knocked down, you just get back up. This book is dedicated to the memory of my parents, Lowell and Louise Winner.

My father had only a ninth grade education, but he didn't let that stop him. His desire to win was tremendous. By age 28, he owned the farm in Michigan where I started my life.

In the late 1940's, he sold the farm and bought some property on a highway to build the restaurant of his dreams. Things went well until the highway began changing into an interstate. The chaos of the new road construction reduced traffic flow and forced my parents into bankruptcy.

Almost immediately, they were back on their feet attitudinally. With very little money, they moved our family of six to Albuquerque, New Mexico to start over.

The day after we arrived, I remember my Dad walking to Highway 66 full of enthusiasm. He continued walking for seven miles toward the center of town until he secured a job at a service station. My mother was able to get a job at a laundry nearby, and all of us kids did what we could to help. By pooling our resources we were able to pay the rent on a very small house. We had no furniture. We slept in our sleeping bags, and cooked on a Coleman stove. The back bedroom where my brother Lee and I slept was cold enough to be used as a refrigerator, and it worked quite well.

Those were tough times for my family, but we shared love and closeness and concern for each other. Even though we were very poor financially, we simply were not poor in spirit because of my parents. As time went on, things improved dramatically.

Many years later, hard times struck again when my dad lost his job. After 17 years with American Car and Foundry, he was laid off. When he realized that his whole future was in jeopardy, he picked up an Alaskan magazine, and out of the clear blue he said, "I'm going to Alaska." Through some contacts my brother had, Dad began talking to someone about taking a job driving a garbage truck. Most people would not even consider working as a garbage truck driver, but my dad never saw it as anything but an opportunity.

My mother tolerated his absence for a few months, then told me to get the truck ready. That meant she was planning to drive a 1965 Dodge crew cab with five-speed standard transmission, no power brakes and no power steering, from New Mexico to Alaska to be with my father.

She called to tell him she was coming. When he told her not to come, she hung up on him because she had already closed out her retirement account and packed the truck. She was determined to go. Moments later, the phone rang, with my father on the line. I only heard my mother's side of the conversation, but she said, "Well, I just want you to understand that nothing in my life is more important to me than you. If I have to sleep on the floor, I will, but I'm coming."

I watched her take that Dodge crew cab with all of her belongings and head down the highway. Because she was only four feet, nine inches tall, she had to sit on a pillow to see through the windshield. She drove that truck through all of the Canadian Rockies, and on to Alaska.

My father worked on the garbage truck for about 90 days before he became manager of the officer's club at Clear Air Force Base. Then he homesteaded, and opened up a snow machine dealership and a Buck knife franchise. Eventually, he and my mother moved to Valdez, where they bought another home and worked until retirement.

No matter what happened, they always kept their dreams in focus, maintained their committment, and moved forward with unquenchable enthusiasm. They lived the concept outlined in this book, and that is why they are such a great inspiration to me.

Thank you Lord for lifting us up
when we were weary. We know without you this book
would not be a reality. To God Be the Glory!

**But those who wait on the LORD
shall renew their strength; they shall mount up
with wings like eagles, they shall run and not be
weary, they shall walk and not faint.**
Isaiah 40:31

ACKNOWLEDGMENTS

I have wanted to publish this book for a very long time. Several years ago, my associate George Thompson said, "Jim, if you really want to write that book, I have a pretty good understanding of computers and how to structure a book, and you have a wonderful grasp of the concept. If you will just audio tape what you think ought to be in it, I'll pull it all together."

In retrospect, I don't think either one of us had any idea what would be involved in writing a book, but this one would not exist without George's total commitment. Working in and around all of his family responsibilities until it was finished, he succeeded where many others have failed. He, in turn, credits his wife, Kathy, for her unwavering support, and the many hours she spent helping him get the words just right.

I would also like to thank my wife, Margaret, for her support. Eight years ago I showed her an early manuscript I put together on my own, and she said, "Sounds great. Let's print it!" Through each draft, she has remained dedicated to her conviction that this concept should be in the hands of thousands of readers where it can impact their lives in a positive and healthy way. So again, thank you Margaret.

As anyone who has ever published a book knows, there are many people assisting at various points along the way. Although there are far too many to name individually, I would particularly like to thank Mike Martin, Bob Sabino, Gary Suboter, and Jean Hamrick for their precious gifts of time, guidance, wisdom, and encouragement. And to the Super Achievers who allowed us to share their lives and achievements, I offer my most profound thanks as well.

Contents

FOREWORD

Our world is changing rapidly. Individuals and companies are struggling to get ahead and stay ahead. People are grappling with adversity on all fronts. Positions that were once secure are no longer secure. Companies are fighting to stay in business. There is much downsizing, restructuring and trauma. And it is a safe bet that the future will continue to challenge us.

This quite naturally leads to the question, "How can we cope with the changes?" Or, better yet, "How can we gain an advantage?"

As many have already discovered, a fundamental component of success is the right attitude. We cannot be customer driven until we are customer focused attitudinally. We cannot produce quality work for our customers unless we are excited about doing so. We cannot attract and retain quality employees without the right attitude towards commitment. We cannot sustain innovation and continual improvement unless we know how to recommit continuously to the challenges of change.

Attitude is critical to success!

Attitude is frequently regarded as an issue that each person must confront individually, yet it is *not* just an individual issue. Groups and teams have attitudes. Corporations have attitudes. And while leadership is an important component in the search for a positive, progressive attitude, evidence suggests that individuals hold the key to a group or company attitude, because the attitude of these organizations is the sum total of the attitudes of its individuals. Because individuals are in control of the group's attitude, they hold the key to success in the quality movement and to organizational success, as well.

Attitude also makes the difference between success — which in today's world means "getting by" — and winning.

Pat Riley, the well-known head coach of the Los Angeles Lakers basketball team, was quoted in a story in *Personal Selling Power Magazine* as follows:

> "The difference between success and winning is in a person's attitude. When I speak before a business audience or talk to my team, I don't talk about success, failure or winning and losing because I don't want to paint that kind of picture. I've always believed that anybody can be successful. If you're a competitive person, and you're striving or aspiring to be the best, then really it's about being that one winner who will somehow find a way to shoot up out of the pack of everybody else who's successful.
>
> "I've found that the people who apply themselves, learn the proper techniques, understand the philosophies, plans, systems and strategies of their organization, take pride in the work and repeat it every single day, are the people who will become skillful and maximize whatever talents they originally brought to the job. The difference between people who are skillful and merely successful, and the ones who win is in attitude. The attitude a person develops is the most important ingredient in determining the level of success."[1]

Throughout history, learned individuals and scholars have shared Pat Riley's viewpoint. William James, known as the father of modern psychology, once wrote that the greatest discovery of his generation was how human beings could alter their lives by altering their attitudes of mind. This is such a profound statement, yet most of us pass through life without ever grasping its significance. Sadder still, very few of us ever learn how to harness our attitude power, even when we recognize it.

Many other authors have written about how attitude makes the difference and about why your attitude should be positive. We totally agree with the philosophy presented in these books, but like many good things in life, they leave us wanting more. They admonish us to have a positive attitude, giving us example after example of how positive attitudes make things happen and how negative attitudes lead to poor results. They teach us to be aware of our attitudes and even give us a few suggestions for improving them. Sadly, however, they leave us on our own for the most difficult part, which is recognizing the point when our attitude is shifting from positive to negative. In other words, they don't really tell us how to control our attitude.

How *do* you control your attitude? How do you recognize when attitude is a roadblock on your highway? The answers are fairly simple but not widely recognized.

We know that much of life follows a pattern because there are patterns in our daily behavior, patterns in our growth and development and even patterns in our grieving process.[2] As we will discover in this book, there is also a pattern to our attitude. This pattern leads us to make instinctive choices. While these choices are frequently good, they can just as easily be destructive. The good news is that we can choose to control our attitude for any desired level of success in life.

This book is dedicated to helping you, the reader, reach an understanding of the attitude cycles that individuals and organizations experience. It will help you see attitude roadblocks and help direct you around them. You will learn about a split-second choice: what choice to make, why it is important and when and how to make it. You will also learn about turning negative situations into positive ones and how to sustain the fundamental attitude pattern necessary for on-going success.

I am confident that this book will make a positive difference in your life.

[1]Gerhard and L.B. Gschwandtner, *Personal Selling Power*, January/February 1991, p. 73

[2]Kubler-Ross, Elizabeth, **On Death and Dying**

Chapter 1

BEGINNINGS

"The longer I live, the more I realize the impact of attitude on life. Attitude, to me, is more important than facts. It is more important than the past, than education, than money, than circumstances, than failures, than successes, than what other people think or say or do. It is more important than appearance, giftedness or skill. It will make or break a company... a church... a home. The remarkable thing is we have a choice every day regarding the attitude we will embrace for that day. We cannot change our past... we cannot change the fact that people will act in a certain way... we cannot change the inevitable. The only thing we can do is play on the one string we have, and that is our attitude. ... I am convinced that life is 10% what happens to me and 90% how I react to it."

From Attitude by Charles Swindoll

Do you ever wonder why some people have unlimited success and happiness in their lives, while others spend much of their time in misery or mediocrity? I do.

As a professional trainer and speaker, I meet a lot of successful individuals. I also work with many people who are not experiencing the success they could. My goal as a trainer is to serve both groups

Like others before me, I have found that attitude makes the biggest difference in our ability to succeed. During the course of marketing my training programs, I discovered a process that can help us take control of our attitude. This book is about the decision-making process all of us experience along the attitude pathways of life. It will help us make good choices, at the appropriate times.

Several years ago, I went to see one of my training customers. As I walked around his business, it amazed me to find that many of his employees had moved on to jobs with other companies. Because employee turnover is common to all companies, I did not pay much attention to this observation at the time. A couple of months later, I noticed the same phenomenon at another organization. This time, my curiosity got the best of me, and I began to conduct some research with people I knew. I asked questions such as, "Why do people change employers and careers so quickly?" and "Why do they change them so often?" Since turnover is an expensive problem for any business, I knew I could help my clients if I discovered methods to reduce the expense.

As I met with more clients, I continued to observe people changing jobs, and I kept asking questions. I spoke with hundreds of people over the months that followed, and I began hearing repetition in their answers. I knew there must be a pattern to the answers, but it was not clear to me at that point.

A couple of years into my research, I faced problems in my own career. It looked as if a job change might be in order for me, too. To prevent making a decision I might later regret, I decided to compare my own situation to those I had been observing. In a sudden flash of insight, I realized that *our attitude cycles in and out of four major phases during*

2

our lives. With this observation, I quickly pinpointed my own position in the pattern. My career was not the problem. It was my attitude! Armed with this new insight, I quickly fixed my attitude by making the simple choice the pattern suggested. I stayed with the career I already had and advanced from there. My crisis was over.

As I continued to evaluate my findings, I was surprised to find that the *type* of career is seldom a factor when people decide to make a job change. The educational background of the employee is not important, either. Gender, age, location, nationality, race — none of these factors seem to matter. With this improved understanding, I began paying attention to the choices other people were making. Clearly, successful people were making the same choice I had made, and not only in their careers, but in all aspects of their lives. This choice, and the process that surrounds it, is the subject of this book. I believe that making this choice consistently is what allows SUPER ACHIEVERS to accomplish phenomenal results, in spite of inevitable obstacles and setbacks.

Roughly half of this book is devoted to an understanding of how our attitude cycles in and out of these four major phases (and their associated subphases). The rest deals with practical application, both on the job and in other areas of our lives. While this material is extremely useful in difficult situations, including career moves, *it is really a tool for everyday use.* These concepts apply to *all* areas of our lives. They apply to marriage, school, community affairs, church and synagogue, hobbies and projects, everyday living — even politics. They will help parents understand and communicate with their children. They will help supervisors understand and communicate with their team members. They will help husbands and wives understand each other and improve their relationships, and they can help YOU understand and control your own actions.

As part of my training activities, I now present these ideas in a variety of workshop settings. During these encounters, heads nod in agreement as we review the various phases and subphases. Afterwards, people say to me, "You've been reading my mail." or "You were looking right into my mind." I have found that these concepts hit home for everyone, without exception. The insight they provide is powerful. Indeed, individuals and companies alike have progressed and accelerated after learning these secrets.

Because the workshop format has proven to be so successful for so many, I have chosen to present this material as if you were experiencing your own private workshop. I will be asking you to mentally place yourself in a traditional job setting long enough for me to explain the fundamentals. If you have never held a job, fear not; you will find it easy to follow along. If your chosen profession is raising a family, simply apply these concepts to that occupation. With two toddlers at home and three grown children, I know from personal experience that the job of raising a family is just as challenging as any other.

Before plunging into the workshop, it will be helpful to understand what I mean by a split-second choice.

A long time ago, I was driving a 1966 Corvette to Farmington, New Mexico. The highway was long and lonely, and the sun was going down. I pushed the gas pedal down firmly, releasing most of the 600 horses under the hood. As the speedometer needle moved forward, I leaned back to relax and let my thoughts drift.

Minutes later, as the car edged over the top of a hill, my reverie snapped. A flock of sheep was standing right in the middle of the highway. I had a split-second decision to make. My options were limited — panic and let fate take its nega-

4

tive course, or take control in a positive way.

Thanks to many years of experience drag racing and driving on dirt tracks, I *automatically* chose the positive approach. I engaged a series of hard braking maneuvers, which sent the car looping and spinning a couple of times. When it finally stopped in a big cloud of dust, my pride was wounded, my brakes were smoking and my cardiovascular system was on full alert. Thankfully, the sheep and I were all alive, and my car was still operative. My split-second decision to act in a positive way had saved us all.

Frequently, when dealing with our careers, our relationships and our daily lives, you and I will find a "flock of sheep" on our attitude highway. The obstacle may not appear as suddenly as the sheep did on my trip to Farmington, but we still have a decision to make. Whether we make a snap decision, or take time to analyze the situation, we experience a split-second point in which the decision is made. As you will soon see, *choosing wisely at those split-second points will strongly influence our success in life. Those split-second choices are crucial.*

This book will help you recognize the critical decision points in your life, career, projects and relationships. It will also help you recognize the habitual decision rule you are using at those critical points. When you can "see" those turning points, the paths they offer and the habitual choice you are making, you can consistently follow the path that is best for you. You can develop a habit that will suit you well.

On my trip to Farmington, I made the right choice, thanks to a well-developed habit. When we make the right attitude choice a habit, it is easier to be a champion for ourselves and for others.

Now, get ready, because it's time to begin reading with EXCITEMENT!

SPLIT SECOND CHOICE

Chapter 2

The First Phase: EXCITEMENT

"I never did a day's work in my life. It was all fun."
Thomas Edison

"If you have a dream, you have everything."
Robert Schuller

Let's begin your workshop by setting the scene. Suppose you are a company president, and you have just hired me. Today is my first day on the job.

Over the last few weeks, you and I met for several interviews. During the first interview, you decided *I could do* the job, that *I wanted to do* the job and that *I would fit in* with your organization.

For the second interview, you asked me to bring my wife, Margaret, along. To validate your initial feelings about me, you had us talk with several other people in your company. They all agreed with your conclusion that I would be *perfect* for the job and that Margaret and I were an excellent team.

With this agreement, the stage was set for you and I to

meet again. In this third meeting, we discussed what you wanted me to accomplish in my new position. You talked about how I was the ideal candidate to achieve great things. Together, we talked about goals and how they would be attained: You painted a picture of my job responsibilities and career opportunities, and I painted a picture of my abilities and commitment. When those two pictures snapped together like the pieces of a jigsaw puzzle, we made the decision to team up. You offered me the job, and I accepted. Then we embellished the picture with images of victory, rewards and glory.

EXCITEMENT PHASE
Dream
Initial Commitment

My future appeared brighter than ever. Beaming with a feeling of euphoria, I went home and told Margaret, "This job is *exactly* what I want. It's the perfect opportunity for me." I also hastened to explain to anyone else who would listen that I was embarking on a magnificent new career, one filled with great promise.

So here I am, feeling like a surfer who just caught the big wave ... a thousand fans on the beach ... the sun bright ... the water bluer than blue ... the beaches whiter than white. With this on-top-of-the-world feeling and dreams of even better things ahead, I have started my new career with you. These dreams of the future sparkle, and they energize all of my activities. There is an energy inside me that is focused on projects and results. I anticipate nothing but good things. I am really EXCITED about the opportunity before me.

As I start this first day, I also feel committed to the job. I'm not sure how long my commitment will last, and neither are you, but we both perceive it's deep enough to cultivate a win-win relationship.

EXCITEMENT

FULL TILT POSITIVE

My engine is revved up, and I'm ready to roll. I can already see the checkered flag waving me on to a victory lap. Because I am truly EXCITED, and because my commitment level is high, any obstacle or complication in the early days of my new career will be easy to handle. I will either leap over, walk around, duck under or just break straight through the difficulty. If things don't happen exactly the way I want them to, I will shrug it off and move on. My attitudinal pendulum is tilted full positive, in a sort of full-speed-ahead position. My enthusiasm level is high, and I am generally very productive.

You may be asking yourself, "Does it really happen this way?" Of course it does. Maybe not always at the level described here, but every time we start a new career, project or relationship, we begin with a positive attitude. Since this phase of our attitude cycle is often accompanied by emotion, enthusiasm and energetic behavior, I have labelled it EXCITE-MENT. We have a dream in mind, and we make a commitment to the career, project or relationship. *All of these feelings and dreams are very real,* and for a while, everything seems to go our way.

Unfortunately, it is difficult for us to keep our *dreams* in clear focus for the long time periods encompassed by careers, projects and relationships. Maintaining a high level of *commitment* over the long term is equally challenging. The hundreds of people I interviewed told me they can usually sustain commitment for 90 days or so, but after six months, it becomes very difficult. So, unless I am a rare exception, my attitude of EXCITEMENT towards my new job with you will last just three to six months. Then it will begin to diminish. And a second phase will strike.

Chapter 3

The Second Phase: FRUSTRATION

"People may fail many times, but they become fail-ures only when they begin to blame someone else."

Anonymous

"If you find a path with no obstacles, it probably doesn't lead anywhere."

Frank Clark

Let's continue the discussion about my job with you. It is now three to six months after I started. The energy of my initial EXCITEMENT is beginning to wear off, and I am beginning to experience more of the realities of my job. It is much more difficult than I anticipated. There are so many things I want to do, and I want to do them well, but things just aren't going the way I expected. I probably don't even realize it, but I'm beginning to shift into a second attitudinal phase. I have labelled this phase FRUSTRATION because of the feelings involved.

For any long-term commitment, and for many short-term commitments, as well, a FRUSTRATION phase follows the

EXCITEMENT phase like night follows day. It's inevitable.

To see how frustration enters our lives, lay this book down for a moment and try this experiment. First, clasp your hands together by intertwining your fingers. Then look down at your hands. Which thumb is on top? The right one or the left? Now, reverse your hands so that the other thumb is on top. Be sure and reverse all of your fingers, too. This second position is very uncomfortable because all of your life, you've been in the habit of putting your hands together a certain way.

If you decide to change that habit (and, by the way, there's no compelling reason to do that, because whether you are left or right thumbed makes no difference), it will require a period of discomfort while you practice the new habit. During that practice period, you have to accept the discomfort. That's what happens in the start-up phase of a new career.

Discomfort is attached to the new habits and skills we are developing. It's a perfectly natural part of the learning process, and it's okay to feel frustrated, especially when we take on new challenges.

IF YOU ARE UNWILLING TO BEAR DISCOMFORT, YOU WILL NOT MAKE PROGRESS TOWARD A DIFFICULT GOAL! YOU MUST COMMIT YOURSELF AND PREPARE TO ACCEPT THE FRUSTRATION.

Back to my career with you: The FRUSTRATION I'm experiencing injects a cloud of confusion into my mind. I feel like a juggler who has picked up one pin too many, and I'm struggling to keep everything moving smoothly. Doubt arrives on the scene, and I find myself asking, "Was it the right decision to come to work for you?" Because of the doubt, my enthusiasm begins to drop. Anxiety comes into play, and my productivity may fall, too.

As my boss, you may not even notice my attitude beginning to slip. If you do, you'll probably just chalk it up to the stress of the job or assume I've got a problem at home. But it begins to dawn on me, vividly, that, "Hey, I'm in trouble." How can this be happening? This was the perfect opportunity for me. You thought so, and so did I.

I'M IN MY FRUSTRATION PHASE!

Let's back up for a moment and examine what just happened in more detail.

I started out EXCITED about my new job with you, and now it's a few months later. The EXCITEMENT phase is beginning to wear off and is being replaced by a FRUSTRATION phase. As you will see, this FRUSTRATION phase can have either four or six subphases, depending on the path we choose to take. But regardless of the path, it starts out with the same four subphases.

1. SHOCK

The first subphase of my frustration experience is SHOCK. I am shocked at the reality of just how *challenging* this job really is, thinking to myself, "Impossible. No way. Just couldn't be this difficult." In this subphase, my attitude pendulum begins to drop away from full positive.

SHOCK

MOMENTUM SHIFTS

13

2. DENIAL

The next subphase is DENIAL. I react defensively to the shock and deny responsibility for many aspects of my commitment to you. It's human nature to do this. I will not admit that I understood *from the beginning* how difficult the job would be. I might even catch myself saying, "Listen, I checked this

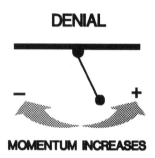

DENIAL

MOMENTUM INCREASES

out carefully, so I can't be responsible for the way I'm feeling." In this subphase, my pendulum is still on the positive side, but it's changing position fast, and my enthusiasm is really beginning to wane. I have given up control of my attitude by denying responsibility for my situation.

3. FEAR

As the frustration continues, and I continue to deny responsibility for my problem, I move into FEAR. I become fearful that I've been trapped and that I won't be able to escape. I start saying to myself, "I expected *some* difficulties, but not all this!"

FEAR

WHICH WAY?

Questions begin to enter my mind, like, "Am I competent? Will I be discovered? What will others think? Did I made a mistake coming to work here? Am I trapped? Is this career what I thought it would be? What will happen if these problems never clear up? Will I ever be okay again?"

What if ... what if ... what if ...?

The resulting fear further inhibits my performance, and my attitude slides into neutral — neither positive nor negative. My focus is diffused and muddled. My commitment drops considerably, and my enthusiasm lacks positive direction. I'm probably not going to cause the company any damage at this point, but it's unlikely that I'll do many positive things, either. Making matters worse, the momentum built up by the natural swing of the pendulum now has my attitude *accelerating towards negative.*

If you leave me in this FEAR subphase for an extended period of time, what emotion will eventually erupt? You're right! I'll become defensive and ANGRY!

4. ANGER

My fears lead to ANGER. In one of man's most natural responses, my systems react defensively, seeking to protect me. I start out angry because *of the way I feel,* and then I look for other targets, like you!

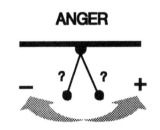

The ANGER subphase is a precarious position for me — a pivotal point. It is where I make a split-second decision, usually out of habit. As noted above, my attitude leaving the FEAR subphase is neutral, but my overall shifting momentum has me headed in the negative direction. Will I continue in a negative direction or stop it and swing back to positive? We'll take up the positive direction in a later chapter. But for now, let's assume momentum carries me to a negative reaction as it frequently seems to do.

NEGATIVE CYCLE

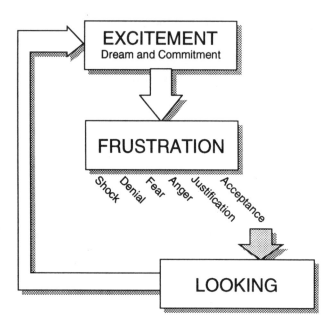

I have just chosen a negative attitude cycle. This decision to "go with the flow" causes me to lash out with negative, outward-directed anger. With outward-directed anger, everyone and everything else is the cause of my frustration — everyone, that is, except me.

The Chinese say, "Four horses cannot overtake the tongue," and that will apply to me. My tongue starts wagging, and I pass out complaints and anger to anyone who will listen:

16

spouse, parents, family, and friends. If there are some generally negative people around, I'll probably start hanging out with them. We'll gravitate towards each other because they will be quick to agree with what I have to say. This will simply reinforce my anger.

Helpful, supportive people — who might understand the frustrations I'm feeling and be in a position to help — may begin backing away from me. I might even push them away without meaning to. As a friend of mine, you might try to help by saying, "Jim, you've got an attitude problem." There's a good chance I would explode and say, "Back off! It's none of your business!"

This anger is born of a type of fear that makes people incredibly defensive. They surround themselves with an impenetrable shield. Even friends are pushed away — friends who, more than likely, will not bring the situation up again.

In the EXCITEMENT phase, I did not see any difficulty in the opportunity ahead of me. Now, I see difficulty *everywhere,* and *very little work gets done.* Plenty of unforeseen problems appear — problems that would have seemed trivial six months ago. Because of my defensive shield, I won't seek any help or assistance. As a result of this negative anger state, I contribute to my problems instead of identifying or seeking a solution. As my anger and frustration continue, I will eventually decide that I'm not going to work here any longer. This decision seems to make all of my problems disappear.

But now I have a new problem: I have to rationalize my commitment to you. Remember when I excitedly accepted your job offer? I start thinking back to our initial job interview, when you and I talked about this opportunity. You probably asked me, "Jim, can you handle this?" And my response was, "Absolutely!" You might have even said,

"What I'm really looking for is a strong-minded self-starter who can take on challenges without a whole lot of support." And I said, "You've got the right person."

JUSTIFICATION

MOMENTUM CONTINUES

To further reinforce your position, you may have added, "You need to understand that in some cases, we won't be there to support you when you need us. You'll just have to keep marching through the difficulty until we can give you some help." My response? "I can walk through hot coals. Don't worry about me."

Now here I am, not wanting to walk through anything that you and I have talked about. I no longer want to fulfill my original commitment to you. To get out of that commitment, I drop into another subphase called JUSTIFICATION.

5. JUSTIFICATION

I *do* realize, subconsciously, that I made a commitment in the beginning. Even so, despite what I may have promised you originally, I have no desire or intention to take care of my obligations. I start compiling a list, mentally or otherwise, to justify my feelings and my decision. I may even seek additional negative input and reinforcement at this point. In this subphase, my attitude pendulum swings completely into the negative area, and it begins gaining speed as I start piling up blame.

First, I would probably blame you, my boss. After all, you got me into this mess. But I won't tell you. I'll just know in my mind that you're part of the cause. I might even mention to someone else that I think you're part of the problem.

FULL JUSTIFICATION

FULL TILT NEGATIVE

To further justify my feelings, I begin to list every thing and every situation and just about every person — *except me*. I might list

... the political changes that cause a certain amount of fear and concern;

... or how the secretaries won't type my reports on time;

... or how the accountants won't let me spend the amount of money I feel is necessary;

... and, of course, the designers and manufacturers are behind schedule in delivering the goods.

Not only that, but the economy has changed ... the job has changed ... my family commitments have changed .. what *we* have to offer is not as good as what *the competition* offers ... and so on. I'll list every negative drawback I can think of, regardless of how small or nitpicking it might be. In my mind, these are valid reasons for not moving forward, although you and I both know that they are nothing but flimsy excuses.

I continue to add to my list of justifications. Like jelly beans on the pan of an old-fashioned set of scales, my pile of excuses gets bigger and bigger and bigger until I finally convince myself to give up. For some people, it only takes three or four jelly beans. Others pile on 15 or 20 before they give up.

This justification subphase *has to be there* because of my original commitment to you. In my mind, I will remain committed to you until I can pile enough reasons on the scale to overcome the weight of that commitment. When I succeed in doing this, ACCEPTANCE sets in.

6. ACCEPTANCE

In the ACCEPTANCE subphase, I decide and mentally accept that I am no longer obligated to meet my original commitment. I am still working for you, and I may continue to do so for years, if you allow me to, but I am apathetic and uncommitted. I'm in a sort of mental semi-retirement state — no gold watches, no testimonial dinners, no celebration — just mental retirement. Everybody knows it. I throttle back, and the rest of the staff picks up the workload. Things move along as usual.

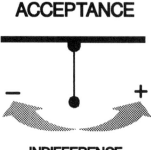

I don't throttle back enough to cause myself to be removed, of course, but most of my real energy goes to activities other than my job. I'll spend more time at the golf course, visiting with friends, or working on my hobbies — anything I can do to remove myself mentally from the frustration of the job and the commitments I made to you.

Accepting my "impossible" situation makes things easier. Releasing myself from my commitment to you eases my burden and relieves the pressure I've been feeling. My hope for a better, brighter future allows the *totally* negative outlook I had in the justification stage to become somewhat mollified. My attitude pendulum can thus ease back to the neutral, uncommitted, indifferent center.

In this subphase, there is no momentum in my attitude at all. At the beginning, I was totally and enthusiastically committed. *Now I am indifferent and much less productive than*

I could be.

A real tragedy is taking place. This was the perfect opportunity for me, remember?

Why isn't it working out?

Why am I throwing it away?

Chapter 4

The Third Phase: LOOKING

---

*"One ship drives east and another west, while the
self-same breezes blow*

*"'Tis the set of the sail and not the gale, that bids
them where to go.*

*"Like the winds of the sea are the ways of fate; as
we voyage along through life,*

*"'Tis the set of the soul that decides the goal, and
not the calm or strife."*

Ella Wheeler Wilcox

To escape my FRUSTRATION, I begin LOOKING for
a way out.

LOOKING PHASE

This third phase, which I call LOOKING, is where I start
to find out what other opportunities might exist for me. It
begins with scanning the want ads, or maybe checking with
friends in the industry. To keep you, my boss, from finding
out about my inquiries, I will do it all in a third-person manner.

I will go about my normal business, occasionally saying, "I have this friend who is looking for a job. Have you heard of any job opportunities lately?" If an opportunity presents itself, I will explore it (discreetly, of course). I might even engage some professional help — in a very low-key fashion — from a recruiter.

I have completely reversed my attitude towards my situation. In the beginning, I was absolutely sure I had entered the most fantastic opportunity in the history of mankind. Now, I am absolutely sure that coming to work for you was the worst decision I ever made. Why? I was lied to, and things were misrepresented. It just didn't turn out the way I expected. (Or so I have convinced myself.)

It is this logic that propels me into LOOKING for a brand new opportunity: another opportunity having the same criteria I thought my position with you offered. Why? So I can get back into an EXCITEMENT phase again.

Psychologists say that we naturally gravitate toward happy situations. People will work to find what makes them happy, and they will make a change, regardless of the cost. Leave me unhappy long enough, and I will clear the decks to make a new start.

It may take time, but I will continue to look. As a matter of fact, I have talked with people who stayed in the LOOKING phase for as long as 20 years. They literally became a ward of their employer. In a large organization, one can hide for a long time. At some point, the organization may even know that you're unproductive, but it's easier to allow you to muddle your way through to retirement than to go through the difficulty of removing you and developing someone else.

Most of the time, I will look to similar industries for my next job opportunity. And it won't be hard to find something because at this point, I have experience. I will eventually find something that seems to meet my needs. I will probably describe it as another ground-floor opportunity — the career position I *should* have had — the most fabulous opportunity one can imagine.

This time, when such an opportunity comes along, I will take extra care in interviewing the company. I will check its background, its financial stability, the people within the company and even the boss (both personally and with respect to company matters). Because of my experience, I now know what I should have asked during my interviews with you. I ask a thousand more questions than I did with you. I make sure to get lots and lots of information. Once I've convinced myself I have the information I need — that this new opportunity is really what I've been looking for and not another mistake — then I make a decision to go with the new company.

I now come back to you, my boss. Before telling you about my decision to move on, I tell you what a great person you are and how wonderful your company is. Why? Because all my life, I've been told not to burn bridges.

Instead of being disappointed, you are relieved. You know I am not productive, and you may have been wondering what to do with me, anyway. So after telling me how much you enjoyed the relationship, and how much I've meant to you, you wish me luck in my new endeavor. You encourage me, saying things like, "Hey, that sounds like a great opportunity. Looks like it's really your cup of tea." Under your breath, you're probably saying, "Thank heaven, this is no longer a problem for me." Of course, your feelings don't really matter, because *I'm sure YOU were the major cause of my problem,* anyway.

Off I go into my new career opportunity. It's important to note that my goals haven't changed — I have merely walked away from my first career opportunity unfulfilled.

But that's okay, because I am back in an EXCITEMENT phase again, telling my family, friends and even strangers what a fabulous, once-in-a-lifetime opportunity I have seized and am holding fast in my grasp. This is it!

My attitudinal pendulum swings back to its positive pole.

Remember, psychologists say that you and I will naturally gravitate back towards a happy situation. Looks like I've found one, doesn't it?

Questions for you to ponder at this moment are, "Will I be okay?" "Is this the one for me?" "Is this the career I have always been looking for?"

Chapter 5

The Cycle Repeats

"Follow me. I'll be right behind you."
Anonymous

Now that I have found another company to work for, and another career, I am excited again. How long will I stay in this "new" EXCITEMENT phase? You are right! Three to six months. Then, suddenly, I will find myself out of EXCITEMENT and back into FRUSTRATION.

Why do you suppose that happens? This was truly *the* opportunity. I checked this company out much more carefully. I asked so many extra questions. How could this possibly happen again?

Let's examine the situation in more detail.

Do you remember the list I used to justify dropping my commitment on the first job? Even though I am honest, chances are good that I did not list myself, or even consider myself to be any part of the problem. I blamed everyone and everything else for my problems.

Well, read carefully, because here is your explanation. Even though I may not be the direct cause of the problem, I am the only person who can do anything about the problem.

That's so important it ought to be repeated. *I am THE ONLY PERSON who can do anything about the problem.* I hold the solutions. I hold all the cards. Even though I cannot control every aspect of every situation, I do have the power to choose a negative or a positive attitude.

I've heard it said that half the people you tell your problems to don't care about them. The other half are glad you have the problem and they don't. Either way, they leave the problem in your lap. *Bottom line: We have to take responsibility for solving our own problems.* When you understand that, you can easily understand that if I am not on the justification list — if I don't consider myself part of the cure or responsible for part of the problem, and if I don't take personal action to make positive changes — the cycle will continually repeat itself.

When the SHOCK strikes this time, do you think it will be greater or less than before? You're right! My SHOCK will be greater. I may be stunned at how two separate companies could be so closely allied in trying to ensure that I fail at everything I ever attempt in life.

Do you think my DENIAL subphase will happen more quickly? Or will it take longer? You're right! It will be immediate. That is how I protected myself last time. So I'll do it again. Right away. I will quickly back out of the stream of responsibility.

The FEAR subphase. Greater or less? You're right again. Tremendous fear! Especially if this is my third or fourth time through the cycle.

A couple of years may have gone by — maybe five. I think to myself, "I cannot continue to change careers (or companies). I just can't. If I continue to do this, I will eventually reach the end of the line, without anything really worthwhile to pursue." Adding to my concern is the fear that at some

point, when I'm older, the job opportunity I'm really quali-
fied for will come along but I'll be competing with a much
younger man or woman. All other things being equal, will I
get the job? Not likely! Even with equal qualifications, and
more experience, I'll probably lose out to the younger person.

The ANGER subphase. Will it be more vivid? Stronger?
More intense? Absolutely. You're right! I immediately surround myself with anger. This way, I can push away anyone
who might help me. It's just human nature to do that: It's a
simple human tendency to push help away. Pride enters, too,
keeping me from asking for help and virtually ensuring that I
will make yet another wrong decision. I may even act like I
know everything, even though I really don't.

Now, JUSTIFICATION. Will it be easier, or more difficult? Right again! It's easier, because everything looks familiar. I simply pull out my old list and place a check mark
by things that apply to my new situation. A handful of new
names and stories are added, and the list is done.

ACCEPTANCE sets in quickly, too. It's the same old story.
I can easily accept the idea of having been sold down the
river again, misled by those I thought were telling me the
truth, lured back into the same old trap.

I immediately shift attitudinally into my LOOKING phase,
where I begin looking for yet another opportunity. If I have
been caught up in the cycle several times, and much of my
life has passed, then this might be my final opportunity to
find what I really want.

Normally, as we are organization or career shifting, we
will stay within our chosen career field, especially if there
are plenty of job opportunities. If the opportunities are scarce,
we may have to relocate to maintain the same career pursuit.
Sometimes, we have to completely shift careers, moving and

changing our line of work. Many people find themselves scanning the want ads on a regular basis. They are constantly shifting and moving. The problem with this is that they never stick with anything long enough to really excel.

I may go through the cycle dozens of times without even realizing that I am swirling through it. Discouraged by repeated FRUSTRATION, I then apply the negative cycle described in Chapter 3 to my own dreams and goals. Goals and dreams I had when I was young now seem unreachable. SHOCKED at this discovery, I begin to DENY that they were ever possible in the first place. With the FEAR of what might happen if I continue to reach, but fail, I become ANGRY at the world.

Along comes JUSTIFICATION to convince me that all of this is somebody else's fault and that I am doing better than most of the people I know. After convincing myself that I have more than most, I rationalize that my opportunities were probably just pipe dreams. JUSTIFICATION makes it easy for ACCEPTANCE to set in: acceptance of easier goals, shallower dreams and lower standards.

This was the story I heard from the hundreds of people I interviewed. As they grew older, they grew "wiser," deciding that some of their original goals and dreams were unrealistic. They reasoned that most of their goals were set by others and that they had never really been personally committed to attaining them. Rather than continuing to develop themselves, they simply reached up, grabbed the high objectives they started out with and pulled them down to their current level of performance. Then, without being truthful to themselves, they said, "I'm satisfied with what I've accomplished. It's all I really wanted, anyway." They went on spending the rest of their lives on a mediocre performance level, a level unnecessarily and unsatisfyingly low.

When a person goes through this cycle time and time again, they will often begin to develop a distorted perception of reality. They start finding fault with people who do well. They criticize our society and systems. They become very cynical, and unhappy, maybe to the point of never being happy again. They say, "Everybody else gets the lucky breaks. I'm a good person, but I never get a break!" Once people decide the rest of the world is lucky and they're not, they usually stay unlucky for the rest of their lives.

THIS CYCLE CAN BE LETHAL. IT CAN CHOKE THE LIFE OUT OF CAREERS, PROJECTS, PERSONAL COMMITMENTS, MARRIAGES, SPIRITUAL GROWTH, FINANCIAL GROWTH, COMMUNITY WORK AND EVEN YOUR HEALTH!

A young man working for me actually taught this attitude cycle in workshops, yet he didn't recognize the stages developing in his own career. He denied that it was true in his case. (Denial is one of the subphases of FRUSTRATION, remember?) He commented that his was a different situation. I must admit there were some differences, but the cycle was still there, choking the life out of his career. Despite the advice given to him and his understanding of the cycle, he made a career change, and then another career change, and the last I heard, yet another one. Meanwhile, a new man took the same territory and excelled.

As you read this, you might be saying, "Wait a minute, Jim. I'll admit there are plenty of people, including many successful people, in the world who have an 'attitude problem,' but they don't seem to be caught up in this lethal cycle. How do you explain that?"

One answer is that many people are simply stuck in the

LOOKING phase, permanently mired in an uncommitted, medium level production mode. They have simply ACCEPTED their FRUSTRATION as a way of life.

There is also a more subtle explanation that I can best illustrate by example. One day, at the beginning of a training meeting with a large oil field organization, a man raised his hand and said, "I want to identify myself. I'm the one that everyone always cuts a wide berth around." (In other words, he was admitting that he had an attitude problem.) I thanked him for his honesty and went on with my program. As we began to toss more ideas around, he made another interesting comment: "In our organization," he said, "it doesn't matter what your attitude is like. If you're skilled enough, you're tolerated." (Here he was trying to say that his attitude problem didn't matter.)

I suppose we can reach certain levels of skill where even a miserable attitude is tolerated because those specialized skills are hard to find. Of course, a miserable attitude doesn't guarantee failure, but it sure increases the odds. The reverse is true, as well. Having the right attitude doesn't guarantee your success, but it does make it more likely.

If you're fortunate enough to be one of those highly skilled people who can't be replaced, then perhaps you can go through life and accomplish a few things, perhaps even most of your financial goals. However, it's unlikely that your relationship with your family and your associates will be ideal. It's also unlikely that you'll reach the top of your field, be promoted into upper management or elected to a leadership position.

A big challenge this country faces is that average, and sometimes even mediocre performance is rewarded quite well. We can do a mediocre job throughout life and yet own a nice home and a couple of cars, have a pretty good lifestyle and raise our children. In other words, it is relatively easy to "succeed" without reaching for one's maximum potential.

After reading this, you might be saying to yourself, "Well, it's too late for me. I'm too old to reach for high goals now." Not true! Many of our world leaders are in their 60s and 70s. Plenty of people are working into their 70s, 80s, even their 90s, setting and achieving new goals all the time.

We choose when to shut it down — which means we also choose when to gear it up.

Colonel Sanders began his Kentucky Fried Chicken chain when he was more than 65 years old. Not only that, but he was turned down by hundreds of restaurants when he first attempted to sell his recipe. Think of the FRUSTRATION he must have experienced! Yet he succeeded in the end.

Inventor Thomas Edison tested thousands of different materials for the filament of his electric light bulb. Many of them failed completely, and yet FRUSTRATION did not send him looking for another profession. Why? The next two chapters will offer some insight into the way these men, and many others, managed to prevail in the face of such attitudinally defeating odds.

At this point, it would be worthwhile to go back and read this chapter a second time, then perhaps even a third. After that, take some time to think through the situations in your life that were similar to the ones described — times when you may have walked away from a commitment unnecessarily. Think about circumstances that were seemingly bad when you left them and how, when looking back, don't seem quite so bad. Were all of the reasons you gave yourself for walking away really valid? Think this through before moving on to the next chapter, and take heart because you can break the negative cycle. We choose the direction of life's journey. It is our choice to make.

Times I Walked Away

_____
_____
_____

	Valid?	
Why I Walked Away	Yes	No
_____	☐	☐
_____	☐	☐
_____	☐	☐

Times I Stayed Committed

_____
_____
_____

Why I Stayed Committed

_____
_____
_____

HOLD IT!

WAIT A MINUTE!

TIME OUT!

WHOA!

STOP!

You mean life doesn't have to be a frustration trap?

SPLIT SECOND CHOICE

Chapter 6

Breaking The Cycle: Your Choice

"Let us grasp the situation. Solve the complicated plot.
Quiet, calm deliberation untangles every knot."
Sir W.S. Gilbert

"Many of life's failures are men who did not realize
how close they were to success when they gave up."
Thomas Edison

To this point, we have been looking at how careers, projects, marriages and many other aspects of our lives can spiral out of control. It's time now to break free of those chains and make some progress.

Not everyone continues to change jobs or says, "That's it, I quit." We must admit that many people do, but not everyone. Some people never seem to quit. Like Colonel Sanders and Thomas Edison, they achieve great things in life, and the roads they are travelling usually aren't any easier than ours. Frequently, there are even more obstacles in their way. How do they do it?

The answer, in large part, is that they avoid the negative side of the cycle.

The negative side of the cycle doesn't have to happen. We can break free from the helplessness. We can break free from the hopeless feelings — that everything we touch dies — that we kill relationships and opportunities and talent. This doesn't have to take place. We can break the cycle. You, me, all of us, have *the liberating power of choice.*

Breaking the counterproductive cycle is similar, in many ways, to the way we avoid collisions. For example, if you knew that backing out of your driveway tomorrow morning would cause you to land right in the path of an unyielding garbage truck, would you do it? If you knew that the garbage truck was going to smash broadside into your car at a high rate of speed, total your car and injure you, would you go out of your driveway in that manner? Or would you find another way to leave your house? *OF COURSE YOU WOULD.* You'd even drive over the backyard fence and through a rock-covered, pothole-infested field to get to work. *YOU WOULD FIND A WAY TO AVOID THAT COLLISION.*

We avoid most collisions in life because we know what to look out for. We can see the obstacles in our way and steer around them.

An attitude collision is not as easy to see coming. It doesn't just show up in front of us. We must learn how to look for it. What we need is some kind of mental guidance system — perhaps a large mental flag, waving and saying, "Danger! Danger! Self, you need to make some different choices and make them now!"

Well, get ready, because it's time to sew that flag.

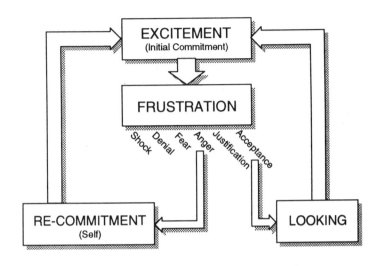

ATTITUDE POWER

To understand how to become part of the solution instead of part of the problem, let's break the cycle down into its component parts.

EXCITEMENT is first. It is the most productive phase. During this phase, our attitude and enthusiasm are high. We get many things done. Our commitment is solid, and things run smoothly. This is where we want to spend more of our time.

Because obstacles always confront us, FRUSTRATION inevitably follows EXCITEMENT in all of our long term commitments and in many of our short-term commitments, as well. It is here, in the subphases of FRUSTRATION, that our attitude begins to slip. Our enthusiasm begins to decline, and our commitment begins to deteriorate. Perhaps this is where we should begin looking for the way out of our atti-

39

tude problem? Ironically, this is exactly what we do.

When we allow FRUSTRATION to overpower us, we proceed to the LOOKING phase to escape. *LOOKING is the phase we want to avoid, because it carries us away from our original objective(s).* We can never totally avoid FRUSTRATION; however, it is here that we can choose to be a part of the problem and complicate things, or we can choose to become part of the solution. This choice belongs to us. No one else can make the decision for us.

To stay EXCITED and avoid LOOKING at other options, the answer must lie in the way we handle FRUSTRATION.

Let's take a closer look at the subphases of FRUSTRATION. Looking at those subphases — shock, denial, fear, anger, justification and acceptance — which one presents a choice to us? Right! ANGER is the only one. *ANGER is the signal that we're about to get into attitudinal difficulty.* We need to see this coming. Just like backing out of our driveway and looking for other cars, we need to be looking for ANGER!

Okay. We know what cars look like, but how do we recognize anger?

The subphases of SHOCK, DENIAL, FEAR and ANGER seem to follow each other naturally and unavoidably. In fact, most of the time, their effects are so subtle that they blend together. How can we identify the exact time and place to make our choices? Fortunately, it is not critical for us to be able to recognize a specific point of time. We need only to be able to recognize the ANGER.

For most of us, ANGER usually manifests itself *in an outward manner.* It can be as simple as a minor feeling of irritation. It could show up with something like gritting our teeth, clinching our fists, cursing a lot or blaming the boss for a problem at work. Or perhaps we find ourselves in a gripe session with fellow workers. This kind of anger is difficult to catch, but we can catch it if we are alert to the signals.

More often, ANGER is expressed in forceful ways, ways which are more obvious and easier to note. We may find ourselves closing the car door a little bit harder. We might slam the door to our house or office when we walk in or slam our books down on the table. We might drop our toothbrush in the morning, then throw it across the bathroom just because we dropped it. We may find ourselves hollering at somebody when we're driving in traffic, or we might snap at our spouse or one of our children. Anything that triggers our temper or puts us out of emotional balance can be the signal flag we're looking for.

We need to be on the alert for these seemingly unimportant signals. These signs of ANGER — some subtle and some not so subtle — can indicate to us early on that we'd better put the brakes on and make the right choice for continued success, or we could be facing a major problem.

But what is the right choice? *The right choice is choosing positively directed anger instead of inwardly or outwardly directed anger. We have to turn our ANGER towards positive solutions to avoid an attitude collision in the outside world.* This is the choice of champions and Super Achievers.

Remember, the ANGER subphase is a precarious position for us. It is the point where we make split-second decisions, and habitual choices. These are learned responses. This means that we will usually respond unconsciously to the stimuli, reacting the way we have been trained to react.

One of the ways we might respond when we feel angry is to direct the anger outward. With outwardly directed anger, everyone and everything is the cause of our problem — everyone, that is, *except us.* As we have seen, this rationalization response is usually unproductive and quite often leads to

JUSTIFICATION, ACCEPTANCE and LOOKING. When we do not take any responsibility for a problem, we are refusing to participate in the solution. We are leaving it for others to resolve.

Another way we might respond is to direct the anger inwardly. *With inwardly directed* anger, we might say, "I know I'm the problem. I'm no good at anything. I'm worthless." This type of approach is self-destructive.

The *best* response, or choice, usually lies in *assuming personal responsibility* for our frustration, then following through by redirecting the energy of our ANGER towards a positive solution. We put blinders on horses so they can only see what's in front of them and thereby avoid distractions. We humans can benefit from a similar strategy. In a sense, we want to blind ourselves to the possibility that a*nything or anyone* could be RESPONSIBLE for the SOLUTION(S) to our problems except us. This will help keep us from simply blaming others for our circumstances and cause us to look toward *real solutions* for our frustration.

Normally, we will want to rechannel our energy by recommitting to our initial goals. This, and other ways of responding will be discussed in the pages that follow. For now, it's only necessary to recognize how POSITIVELY FOCUSED ANGER can be one of the most powerful tools we have to keep ourselves marching towards our goals for ourselves and our families.

I didn't completely understand how anger could be used in this positive, productive way until I reflected on my experience with rheumatoid arthritis.

Many years ago, I was serving in the Marine Corps and stationed in Japan. I was a long way from home, family and friends. For three months, I found myself locked in a full body cast, getting weaker each day and watching my weight drop by more than 40 pounds. My doctor told me, "Jim, you need a medical discharge. You're never going to walk again. Even if you manage to walk for a while, you will be crippled at 35 and confined to a wheelchair from that point forward." I didn't know what to think. It looked as if the doctor might be right. But somewhere deep in my spirit, I just knew I could not allow that to happen. I didn't want to be shipped back to the naval hospital in California, either. He continued to push me toward a medical discharge, and I continued to refuse the transfer.

Eventually, I was sent to therapy, where I consulted with an elderly Japanese physical therapist. I wish I could remember his name because he represented a wonderful, refreshing experience for me. In broken English, he asked me, "You want walk?" I looked at him in shock. No one else had asked that question. They had only told me that I would not walk. Not knowing anything else to say or do, I just nodded my head affirmatively. He lit up with a smile, and said, "Okay. You walk." I'll never forget that moment.

That day started a six-month process of physical therapy. I actually had to learn to walk all over again. But what a joyful experience. His daily encouragement focused not on where I was, but on where I would be if I continued to make the right choices. So, I kept making those choices, as painful and difficult as they were, and exactly 13 months from the day I entered the hospital, I walked out on my own two feet. I could not do a deep knee bend and get back up without support, but I was able to walk.

The doctor refused to give me light duty and sent me back to Okinawa, instead. He was still convinced I could not get well. My anger was so great that I wanted to knock that doctor's head off, but privates do not strike captains in the Marine Corps without winding up in the brig. He must have felt that I would give up and ask for the medical discharge. I decided to prove him wrong. Every morning, I got up early to exercise and strengthen my legs. Six months later, I was marching 15- and 20-mile forced marches successfully. And today, well past the 50-year marker, I'm still able to walk and run.

The tragedy of this experience was that I went through the pain of recovery to prove the doctor was wrong, not to get well. As sad as that may be, it taught me a great lesson. I learned that anger, focused with a positive intent, is one of the most powerful tools we have to make changes, to exercise choices, to turn our dreams into reality. Used in a positive way, we can focus the energy of our anger to achieve whatever we need to achieve.

As noted above, we'll be discussing more about how to focus our anger in a positive way in the chapters that follow. Right now, it's important to add another point. *We can't always see anger coming. We might not even recognize it when it arrives.* Sometimes, we blow right through ANGER into JUSTIFICATION, which is where we really start blaming others for our problems. That's okay, in fact it's even good, because *it offers us yet another opportunity* to make the right choice. If we can't catch our anger *on the front side* of the decision point, we can still catch it *on the back side.* Then all we have to do is back up a little bit and steer our attitude in the right direction.

In summary, if we can see the negative use of anger coming, or catch ourselves directing anger at other people and organizations, then we can refocus and redirect its energy. We can catch our attitude pendulum before it swings to the negative, and send it back to the positive. Accomplishing this will keep our attitude positive, our enthusiasm channeled in the right direction, and our commitment level high.

You are probably saying to yourself, "Okay, fine. I see how to catch myself, and I see how ANGER can be a positive force. But what can I do to redirect it towards a positive solution? How do I redirect my attitude? How do I drive my pendulum back towards the positive?"

Remember Colonel Sanders? What do you think he did when he was turned down for the hundredth time? What do you think Thomas Edison did each time he tried a filament that didn't work? Here's a clue:

When we make the right choice during the anger subphase, our problems are half solved.

We can avoid the deadly LOOKING phase if we want to. It is our choice. We can travel through a fourth phase, instead, and totally bypass the LOOKING phase like other successful people do. In the next chapter, I will show you how right choices make this cycle work for you instead of against you.

Before moving on to the next chapter, this would be a good time for you to stop and think for a moment about the times in your own life when you were up against tough odds. Did you respond by directing your anger in a way that made positive results take place? There are probably many cases where you took positive directional control. I am confident in that assertion because if you were not already a winner, you would have stopped reading this book long ago.

TIMES I USED POSITIVE
ANGER AND SUCCEEDED:

_____

_____

_____

_____

_____

_____

_____

_____

_____

_____

_____

Chapter 7

The Fourth Phase:
RECOMMITMENT

"All of the significant battles are waged within the self."

Sheldon Kopp

OKAY, IT'S SOLUTION TIME.
BUT REMEMBER, YOU ARE THE
ONLY HOLDER OF THE KEY.

YOU, AND ONLY YOU,
ARE RESPONSIBLE FOR YOUR
ATTITUDINAL DIRECTION IN LIFE.

Let's start the cycle all over again. We'll keep the same set of circumstances, but this time, we will direct ourselves down the POSITIVE path of the cycle.

You're my boss again, and we start off in the same way. You interview me three times, and you also interview my spouse. You offer me the job, and I accept it. With my acceptance comes my initial commitment. I don't know how long my commitment will last, and you don't know, either, but it looks like a win-win situation for both of us. I start to work for you, seeing my job as a great opportunity. Things go well for a period of time.

This EXCITEMENT phase is "just right" and doesn't need to change. At the beginning of any commitment, project, career or relationship, we will find some measure of excitement. If we cannot find some value and personal reward at the beginning, we should not, and probably would not, start the process.

Also note the positive way that I see the job: I see it as a great opportunity. This positive dream of my future can and will help me get back up on the tracks after I fall off.

Reality doesn't change, either, and within three to six months, I will shift into a FRUSTRATION phase for some reason. SHOCK will strike. I will DENY responsibility. FEAR will loom. ANGER is ready to strike, too, but this time, I will respond differently. (Remember, we will never be able to eliminate FRUSTRATION, but positive choices at the moment of truth can direct our energy favorably instead of unfavorably.)

So, here I am. I'm SHOCKED at the difficulty of the job. I DENY it's my responsibility, and I shift some responsibility to you, my boss. At this point, I become FEARFUL it won't work out and that I might fail. ANGER strikes, but instead of directing the ANGER in an unproductive way, I say, "Self, you've got a problem." And at that point, I take all of this powerful energy — one of the most powerful energy forces we have — and I focus that energy towards a solution instead of complicating the problem. The right decision is to choose personal responsibility for my own situation, my own attitude, my own destiny — to take charge and make positive changes.

POSITIVE CYCLE

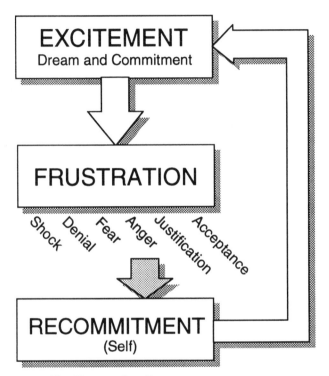

EXCITEMENT
Dream and Commitment

FRUSTRATION

Shock Denial Fear Anger Justification Acceptance

RECOMMITMENT
(Self)

Re-Dream the Dream
Short Term Goals
Outside Opinion

I begin a more productive, alternative phase of my journey during this split-second decision in the ANGER subphase when I say, "No way. Not for me. This is not going to be outwardly directed ANGER. *I'm not going to blame other people* I'm not going to feel sorry for myself, either, but I am going to look inside of myself and ask, 'Where or what can I change? How can I strengthen my position? How do I get *myself* back on track and back into another EXCITEMENT phase?'"

By taking on the responsibility of becoming a part of the solution, I've made a very positive and assertive step towards dealing with my frustration or its cause. And there's a bonus: Admitting that I am at least partly to blame for my problems has a cleansing effect. I'll feel better right away just knowing that someone is going to take responsibility for solving the problem. My next move is to get back into an EXCITEMENT phase.

How?

Starting with my foundation of hope, optimism and courage, I redirect the negative energy my FRUSTRATION is producing. I channel this energy in a way that gets me back into the positive EXCITEMENT phase, where I can refuel the booster rockets of my attitude. Once there, I can also productively search for, and help construct, solid solutions for any *real* frustration I am experiencing. We'll talk about what that means in the chapters that follow.

To get myself back into a new EXCITEMENT phase, there are several simple things I do. They all involve the same general action concept, which is to *recommit myself to my vision and my goals*. This is why I have labelled the fourth phase RECOMMITMENT. I have found three helpful steps in this RECOMMITMENT phase:

1. RE-DREAM THE DREAM

In many ways, people are like the old-time, steam-driven locomotives of the 19th century. Remember the way those engines just kept chugging down the tracks? Until they ran out of steam, that is. For humans, dreams are the fuel of the Enthusiasm Engine that powers our human locomotive. To carry a full head of steam at all times, we need to keep our mental engine full of dreams.

Whenever I find myself in the ANGER subphase and running out of steam, my first step toward correction is to sit down and ask myself, "Why did I start this commitment or career or relationship (or take on this opportunity or project) in the first place?" The initial thoughts I have concerning a commitment are healthy, positive, inspiring and uplifting. Remember chapter one and the EXCITEMENT phase? Remember the dreams I had and how I saw that particular career as the perfect career for me? Now is the time to review those thoughts.

I ask myself:

"What was my dream?"

"Why did I choose to commit myself?"

"Why was the excitement there?"

"What result did I want from that situation or dream?"

"Who else was excited about it?"

I make sure I think back and re-experience the positive feelings I had, the vision and sounds of success, the reasons and motives behind everything I chose to do at that time.

Each time I mentally revisit those dreams, I cause my finish line, or victory party, or desired reward, to look better than it did before. Usually, this thought process alone is enough to renew my spirit, cancel out much of the FRUSTRATION I am experiencing and propel me right back into a new EXCITEMENT phase.

Almost every book or tape on attitude or achievement tells us to believe in a successful end result. They suggest making mental pictures, or visualizing each step of our intended activity in order to strengthen our performance. This is what super achievers and champions do. They re-dream their dream frequently as part of their training and competitive conditioning. Virtually all Olympic gold medal winners describe their state of mind just before and during competition as one of simply living out their dream. This human ability to see a desired goal and then make it happen is one of the most powerful aspects of human motivation.

As long as the dream is clear, alive and healthy, our attitude helps move us toward the achievement of that dream. When the dream gets cluttered, foggy, fuzzy or hard to see, then we start focusing on the obstacles in front of us. When that happens, our attitude becomes a faulty part of our internal circuitry and helps burn us out instead of moving us forward. Our EXCITEMENT begins to diminish, and FRUSTRATION replaces it. It is critical for us to keep our dreams clearly in front of us.

You've heard the old saying, "He couldn't see the forest for the trees."? Here's another experiment for you. Find a large, wall-mounted mirror, and put the book down. Hold your right hand out to the right, and extend your left hand to the left. Looking in the mirror, focus both eyes directly on your right hand. Now, without losing focus of your right hand, look at your *left* hand. Be sure to keep looking at your right hand! Of course you can't do that. **It's impossible to focus on two things at once.**

As a wise hunter once said, "A dog can't chase two rabbits." We must choose to follow the dream, not the difficulty. If we focus on the difficulty, we will spend all of our energy fighting instead of progressing.

How about trying another experiment? Find a penny. With your left eye closed, put the penny between your thumb and forefinger, and hold it close to your face in front of your right eye. What do you see? The penny. And that's all we're going to see. When we focus on the difficulty of the situation, we will not see the goal any more, and we will stay frustrated.

Our choice has to be to pull that penny aside. Why? When you pull the penny aside, what do you see? The whole world is in front of you. Don't let insignificant, petty circumstances act like that penny and block your vision from the wonderful opportunity you and I have in this life. The human race has more worthwhile projects and goals in front of it than ever before. They may be challenging to see, but they are there, and they can belong to you when you make the right choices.

A wise gentlemen once said that "enthusiasm is the flywheel that carries your saw through the knots in the log." I interpret this to mean that we need to redream our dream every time we encounter a knot in our life, every time we encounter an obstacle that seeks to slow down the progress of our saw.

2. SHORT-TERM GOALS

Sometimes, my FRUSTRATION runs deeper than thoughts of success can overcome. When I need additional strength, I take a second step to get back in an EXCITEMENT phase. I call this step "short-term goals."

One of the reasons FRUSTRATION has taken a strong hold of me is that I haven't experienced much success lately. Frequent success can make it easy to ignore occasional frustration, but repeated failures and setbacks have demoralized me to the point where I see only more failure in my future. I'm very discouraged, and that is why I am LOOKING to escape. Have you ever suffered through a success accomplishment drought like this?

I have to reverse this process. I need some success right away. The best way to get some is to start with a small success and build from there. I look for a place where I can set a simple, short-term goal and cause some success to happen.

Psychologists say that when we accomplish something, our brain emits an endorphin. It's like a pure form of morphine, and we wind up with a real lift in our spirit. What I need is to get my spirit lifted.

One way to guarantee some short-term success is to set up a series of one-hour projects — one for each day of the week or several for one day — that are fail safe. To give you an example of how simple this might be, let's assume that our car is so filthy we hate to admit it's ours. There may be some old candy wrappers inside, or a half-eaten apple underneath the seat, and maybe the internal odors are starting to overwhelm us. So we say, "That's it. Come Saturday morning, I'm going to wash that car."

At 10 a.m. on Saturday, we take on the project. We wash the car. We wax the car. We clean the mag wheels. We scrub the tires. We wipe newspapers on the windows to get the glass sparkling clean. We polish the chrome. We shampoo the carpets. We vacuum the trunk, and when we are through, the car looks better than the day we drove it off the showroom floor.

It's been a couple of hours, and we're hot and sweaty. We decide to go down to the convenience market and pick up a soda. When we get in the car, it seems to start more easily. It seems to run better. It seems to shift more smoothly. I've even had people tell me a clean car gets better gas mileage, because as the wind flows over the clean, unrestricted area of the car, it has less resistance. Ever felt like that? This is an example of how multiple benefits can stem from one success.

But let me ask you, what really changed? That's right. We changed. We set a goal and accomplished it. We successfully finished a project and got endorphins to lift our spirit. And with each successive project, we will find ourself winning and accelerating back into an EXCITEMENT phase.

Short-term success can be measured in terms of hours or even minutes, as well as in terms of large or small accomplishments. When working in a sales capacity, I can set a goal to make 10 prospect calls in a given timeframe, then get on the telephone and do it. If I'm experiencing frustration in my communications with someone, I can set a goal to reestablish or enhance communication, then call the person I'm having difficulty with in order to work toward achieving my goal right away. It's easy to set and achieve short-term goals.

Ideally, the short-term goals I choose should be related to my overall goal. It can really benefit me to clean my car when it helps move me forward towards a larger, more important objective, like working towards a sale with a customer who will be impressed by the cleanliness of my automobile.

What's the bottom line? Some action is needed to provide immediate success — to allow me to progress toward my dream. Success will help convince me that things are eventually going to work out in my favor. Success will lead to more success and get my pendulum swinging back in the positive direction.

The positive feelings that result from fresh success are usually enough to accelerate me right back into EXCITEMENT. But once again, I am the only one who can make things happen. No one else can take action for me. I must make that choice for me, and you must make it for you.

3. OUTSIDE OPINION

What if re-dreaming the dream and reaching some short-term goals are not enough? Whoa! Hold it! You mean, that may not be enough? Sorry to disappoint you, but the answer is yes. Sometimes, we need to take a third step. In many cases, this is the most difficult step to take.

Let's suppose that short-term projects lift me up some, but the FRUSTRATION is now so deep that I can't get myself back into that state of sustained EXCITEMENT where I'm really productive. This is when I go into my third step. I need a special person to give me some good, objective advice. I call it an "outside opinion."

I must look for the right person. *Most people simply will not do.* I need to find someone I can trust, someone who is impartial, someone who can give me sound advice. Ideally, I need someone who has successfully mastered a situation similar to mine.

Let me first identify some people who probably will not be helpful.

In my younger days, before she passed away, I might have called my mother. She loved me, and would do anything I asked her to do. If I were to call my mother, I would probably say, "I'm not very happy right now. I'm having a terrible time with my career, and things are not going well. The company is not doing what they promised to do. They're not treating me the way I thought they'd treat me. I'm not growing as fast as I want to grow. Things aren't changing like I want them to change. Mom, I'm so frustrated I can't stand it. Sometimes I want to just sit down and cry about how bad things are."

A mother will sympathize with her offspring. She will likely agree with everything I say. She might even make a phone call to you, my boss, and tell you to get off my case.

If I really sound depressed and frustrated, Mother might possibly say, "Quit. Get out of there. You're too talented for that. Why put up with it? You know you can do anything you want to. You were looking for a job when you found that one. They don't appreciate you."

But is quitting the answer? It may be, and we'll discuss that possibility later. For now, let's assume that quitting is not in our best interest. Since I don't want to quit, my mother's no help.

Who else can I talk to? I could call a couple of good friends or perhaps talk it over with my spouse. Would that be a wise thing to do?

If I call someone who loves me, they'll ask, "What's wrong?" I'll tell them my problems. Because they love me and are sympathetic to my feelings, they'll probably agree with everything I say. They may even take my side and join me in blaming the company or my boss for my difficulty. As a result, they're no help.

Of course, the only information they have is what I tell them. They naturally join my side because they only have my half of the story. During the early part of my career, I recall telling my wife all the things I was asked to do that I didn't like, but I never told her how right those things were for me after I did them. As a result, she only got half of the picture, and there was no way for her to feel good about my career the way I did because she didn't have all the information. And your friends won't, either. It's not likely we'll tell them the whole story because if we understood the whole story, we probably wouldn't be where we are attitudinally. If we understood completely, we wouldn't need their help.

And as my mother did, my spouse and my friends may even suggest that I take the wrong path to solve my problem.

That wrong path would be slipping out the back door like a thief in the night. Worse yet, I might agree and take a walk on that path, because it's easier to blame someone else and quit than it is to accept responsibility and lead myself out of trouble.

When I am locked in the FRUSTRATION phase, I can be so full of fear that my attitudinal clock will stop keeping correct time. It may even begin ticking backwards. I'm not thinking straight. Nothing I decide in this state of mind will be correct because I'm running down a blind alley. I think someone may even be chasing me. I'm running anyway, as fast as I possibly can.

F.E.A.R.
(FALSE EVIDENCE APPEARING REAL)

Fear such as that can only be destructive. But as the Chinese say, nothing is to be feared; it is only to be understood. I need to find someone who can help me understand. If I can't talk to my mother, my spouse or my friends, who can I talk to? I need to find someone who will be empathetic, not sympathetic — someone who can understand how I feel, but who won't actually share those feelings. This kind of person can help me out of the pit without falling in there with me.

THE BOSS

The best person to discuss the problem with may be my boss. After all, we both have many of the same goals in mind. Also, the expense of replacing me might be far greater than the cost of helping me make it through this difficult time. More likely than not, my boss will be thrilled to give me the support I ask for and need. So I must have the courage to approach my boss for help.

But what if I'm finding it difficult to talk to my boss? Perhaps I've tried before without success, or perhaps I don't feel like the boss will be able to help. Perhaps I don't think the boss can be objective and/or impartial. What can I do?

The Chinese have another useful proverb: "If you want to succeed, consult three old people." This is very appropriate advice for my situation. I need to find someone I respect, admire and trust. It needs to be someone who can be empathetic and put themselves in my shoes, yet give me advice that's positive and not negative; someone who might even tell me, "Hit the streets. Make some more calls. Get back in there. Talk to your boss. Hit it harder. Go to school. Reeducate yourself. Be flexible." In short, it needs to be someone who can wake me up to reality and set me straight on course again, someone who will encourage me to stay until I fulfill every single commitment I made. Let's count ourselves fortunate when we have a boss, spouse, parents or friends who tell us in kind, or perhaps even in firm ways to get a grip, quit whining and get back to work.

The real secret lies in getting advice from someone who is not emotionally involved with you or your problem. It may be someone higher up in your company or organization, or perhaps a personal friend who has it all together. It may even be a person in another organization that you seek out by asking around. People like this are often called mentors, or red-flag partners. If chosen carefully, they can usually provide objective and impartial help.

RED-FLAG PARTNERS

A red-flag partner is a person who knows my situation well and will straighten me out when I need it. He or she can be an impartial friend, an objective co-worker or simply a help-ful person in a position similar to mine — a person who knows which questions to ask. (Make sure they read this book so they'll know.)

Red-flag partners are generally there for emergencies, to help us get past a crisis. When you raise the red flag, your partner is there to listen and to help. After listening to your concerns, this partner shakes you awake, takes you back to the first step under recommitment and says, "Okay, let's talk about your dream. What are you trying to accomplish?"

Your red-flag partner controls the conversation with ques-tions, and you allow it to happen. They listen while you ex-plain again what you are trying to accomplish, with even more vivid detail, more clarity and more color. (The purpose here is to get that dream solidly back into your mind where it can pull you forward.) Then, he or she will walk you through step two of the recommitment process and help you set short-term goals. (Be sure to write the goals down, and ask your partner to hold you accountable for achieving them. Better yet, hold yourself accountable for the results, then send a thank-you note or gift to your partner.)

Your red-flag partner may also be able to suggest some creative ways of eliminating your frustration. Since you are in an emotional state, and he or she can remain objective, this person may be in a better position to see the forest instead of the trees. We need to listen carefully to objective, caring people. Pushing our emotions aside for a moment may be difficult, but that's what we need to do.

Since FRUSTRATION is inevitable, wouldn't it be a good idea to find a red-flag partner early, before FRUSTRATION strikes? Of course it would. It's best to identify a red-flag partner when both you and your partner are in EXCITEMENT phases. It's also good to make very strong commitments to help each other in times of difficulty and to have more than one such partner. And if they aren't available at the moment you need them, they know to get back with you quickly if you leave a message that it's about a serious communication.

MENTORS

Counselor. Guide. Teacher. Tutor. These are all synonyms for the term mentor. Each one suggests that a mentor will point us in the right direction and help us learn.

Students of the martial arts often refer to their instructor or master as "sensei." Sen means "before," and sei means "born." Thus, the literal meaning of the term is "one who is born before." While the instructor is often an older individual, the real meaning of being "born before" lies in the wisdom the master possesses. Presumably, the master has experienced what the student is going through and has successfully mastered the task. At least he or she should know how to help the student master it.

A mentor can be a very powerful ally during our periods of FRUSTRATION. Since this person is "older and wiser," he or she should be able to guide us through the forest of FRUSTRATION and back into the green grass clearing of EXCITEMENT. Remember, the best mentor is someone who has been there or has successfully navigated the rough waters we are facing. That's where our best advice will ultimately come from. By seeking out people who have avoided frustration, surprises and negative experiences, we can learn how to avoid problems ourselves.

The right mentor provides guidance, direction and, most importantly, wisdom — a strong and steady hand — a rock or shelter for stormy times. Sometimes, just asking ourselves what the mentor would say is enough to help us. No matter how much experience we have, a mentor is a good thing to have. Nowhere is this better demonstrated than in the martial arts, where even the masters have masters.

The objective advice I receive from a mentor or red-flag partner and the encouragement given to me are almost always enough to turn my commitment, my enthusiasm, my attitude and my excitement around. Chances are high that you won't need to leave that company, situation, project, marriage or relationship. Why? Because everything you ever dreamed of is still there, just like in the beginning. You are merely camouflaging it with negative thinking born of FRUS-TRATION.

RECOMMITMENT STRENGTHENS US

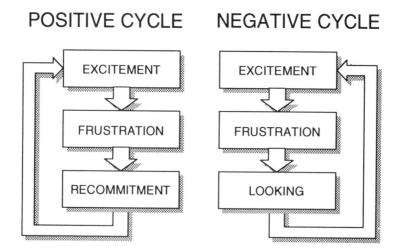

Once we make a positive move out of FRUSTRATION into RECOMMITMENT and rise above a particular situation, is it likely that the same set of circumstances will put us back into FRUSTRATION? No, it's not likely. The same set of circumstances cannot stop you; however, a variation of those circumstances could have another frustrating impact. But having successfully mastered the first situation, we are in a better position to work our way out of the second.

Each time we go through the cycle, each time we hit that wall of frustration and we fight through it, we get stronger and stronger and stronger. Of course, if we don't fight through it, we get weaker and weaker and weaker.

The net result of the four-phase cycle is this: We can repeatedly follow the negative cycle, getting weaker and weaker, eventually having to lower our expectations in life. Alternatively, we can repeatedly **CHOOSE the positive path of the cycle and continuously get stronger.** Through continuous recommitment, we can begin to reach out and accomplish greater goals and greater expectations, some higher than we ever dreamed possible. We can use our knowledge of this cycle to our advantage.

IT'S YOUR CHOICE!

We know that FRUSTRATION is a natural part of living and part of the learning process, so we cannot avoid it completely. Am I able to avoid FRUSTRATION after all these years of working with the concept? Absolutely not. I try to move quickly on to recommitment, using the frustration as a strengthening process. Each time my runway is bombed by frustration, I rebuild it with the stronger concrete of renewed commitment and enthusiasm.

Every time frustration slaps us in the face, we ought to say, "Thank you. Thank you! This is an opportunity to make some real progress, and now is the time to get started." Plunging in and recommitting with enthusiasm kicks us right back into a high level of excitement and productivity. As Confucius said, "Men's natures are alike: It is their habits that carry them far apart." *Recommitment is one of the best habits we can form.* It is a habit that will carry us to great horizons.

FRUSTRATION is merely a temporary storm passing through our lives, while EXCITEMENT is the rainbow in a clear blue sky. FRUSTRATION always passes back into EXCITEMENT, but unlike the rage of foul weather, it's our choice as to when. Cycling back into EXCITEMENT makes us feel good. And as is the case with the weather, we will always be able to see and be awed by the beauty of the rainbow after a storm.

STOP!

STOP!

STOP!

Do yourself a favor, and read this chapter two more times.

First time   ☐
Second time   ☐

Then find a red-flag partner and a mentor.

Red flag partner   ☐
Mentor   ☐

NOTES ON MY EXPERIENCES:

_____

_____

WHAT I HAVE LEARNED:

_____

_____

SPLIT SECOND CHOICE

Chapter 8

Walk Away On
Success

"You can't turn your back until you've faced it all.
Take my word, you're leaving too soon."
Words to *You're Leaving Too Soon*
by Barry Manilow and Enoch Anderson

IS IT TIME TO QUIT?

In the last chapter, I suggested that the way to maintain a positive attitude is to keep yourself in an EXCITEMENT phase as much of the time as possible. We do this by redirecting our emotions to keep the FRUSTRATION phase as short as possible and then recommitting ourselves to our original plans. This works well for most situations and is, in large part, responsible for the success achievers experience. But is it the right course of action all the time? What if recommitment simply will not work?

Let's answer those questions by starting with another question. Is every job, career, marriage or relationship you've ever had, or will have, worth saving? Certainly not. There are times when it is advisable to quit, but only after you have objectively analyzed the situation and have decided that this is truly in your best interest.

There will be times in your life and your career when you will be unable to recommit to a given set of goals. Perhaps things have changed since you set the goals, or perhaps your goals have changed. As is often said, the only thing certain about life is uncertainty. Even well-chosen dreams can have an element of uncertainty when we begin. A statistician would describe this by saying that in a small percentage of cases, things will go wrong.

If an objective and unemotional analysis shows that your goals are no longer compatible with those of the project, marriage, organization or relationship, then it may be time to leave. If the company you're working for cannot, or will not, fulfill the needs that you have, or if your mentor says that you have done all that you could, then move on to something else, but leave in a positive manner. Fulfill your obligations, and then leave. Leave through the front door, in the middle of the day, with the sun shining on your brow and causing a slight tan. Leave knowing that everyone in the organization is praising your performance and saying, "We lost a good person, a person who did everything they promised to do before they left." Leave feeling good about yourself for doing it right.

In a world as complex as ours, there are many ways to find ourselves in a no-win situation. Some of these would include:

1) You're in over your head.
2) Your boss isn't rational.
3) Your goals are not compatible with those of the organization.
4) Your beliefs and/or values are not compatible with those of the organization.

5) You have talent, and you're in a dead-end job.
6) An opportunity more compatible with your goals and dreams comes along.
7) It is simply the wrong time: You are right for the job, but the relationships just aren't complementary.

Obviously, it isn't possible for me to identify every type of no-win situation you may face. What is important is to be able to recognize them and then to know what to do when you find yourself in one of those situations. At times, you may simply need to get away as fast as possible. A person in an abusive relationship is one case in point. At other times, it may be to your advantage to wait for a strategic opportunity to leave.

Most people would agree, however, that the best time to leave a project or career is when you can say, "My work here is done. It's time for me to ...

... take on a bigger challenge."
... move up to something new and different."
... accept that promotion."

These are all seen by others as positive changes in your life. On your next job interview, you will have something to speak of proudly. Finding a rewarding job will be easier.

Contrast that previous set of statements with these: "I'm leaving because ...

... they never do things right."
... I couldn't get any help from them."
... I'm moving on to the job I always wanted anyway."

In these cases, the next job interview is more challenging and less likely to have the positive result you want. To sum it up, the best advice I can give you is to stick it out, and leave on a positive note. Leave at the peak of your career. Go out a winner!

GETTING THINGS TO CHANGE

You might be thinking, "I can understand why I would want to stick things out if I'm the one that's causing the problem. But why should I hang around if I'm not the one to blame?"

The simple answer is character. If we always do the right thing, then our character remains unassailable and invulnerable to attack. We will be able to truthfully say, "I did the right thing. I am a winner." The alternative is to falsely rationalize and say, "I did my best. It was his or her fault that things didn't work out." Playing the blame game is characteristic of losers.

Western novelist Louis L'amour was quoted as follows: "There have always been hard times. There have always been wars and troubles — famine, disease and such-like — and some folks are born with money, some with none. In the end it is up to the man what he becomes, and none of those other things matters. It is character that counts."[1]

How many people commit a small crime, go on the run, then eventually turn themselves in? Isn't it because of the guilt resulting from not paying the price, not making the right choice about that mistake and having to fight their way through it? They're not able to live with it. If we run, we're going to have the same problem in our lives.

When we refuse to take responsibility for our commitments, they are going to gnaw at our character, and gnaw and gnaw. One day, they may take us down for the count. It's very important that we fulfill the commitment. Then we can look at ourselves in the mirror and honestly say to the man or woman in the glass, "You did everything you could."

There may also be times when you can get things to change

in such a way that you can then recommit to your original goals. This would allow you to stay and fulfill all of your dreams. In the next several chapters, I will discuss ways to deal with frustration and what we should do as an employee or an employer.

ARE YOU AFRAID TO DISMOUNT?

An ancient saying reads, "He who rides a tiger is afraid to dismount."

Many of us find ourselves in situations where we feel we cannot walk away, no matter what. We delay making the decision to leave or making the decision to confront the situation head on. This is quite natural. We know what to expect if we do nothing, but we don't know what to expect if we take a leap.

Well, we can't steal second base by keeping our foot on first. And we can't make an omelette without breaking some eggs. Since FEAR usually results from nothing more than inadequate information or education, the answer lies in taking action to learn more about our alternatives.

We can begin by identifying each alternative we have (leave now, stay without changing, make some changes), then gathering data that allows us to decide which course of action will best serve ourselves and any others involved. After we have assured ourselves that we've chosen the best alternative, it's time to take a leap of faith.

Remember that the strongest steel is forged in the hottest furnace. So whether we decide to dismount or to stick it out, it often means plunging into a hot furnace. This will certainly be uncomfortable for a while; however, many times, greatness rises out of the ashes of adversity. So let's resolve to take the action we and our mentor feel is best.

Despite what some people say, it *does* matter whether we win or lose, but it *also* matters how we play the game. Make it happen! *Carpe diem!*[2]

[1]*Reader's Digest*, October 1995 — "Points to Ponder Section," p. 201 — reference is to Chancy (Bantam)
[2]Translation: Seize the day!

Chapter 9

Dealing With
FRUSTRATION

"So, you think you know everything, but you don't know the difference between an inconvenience and a problem. If you break your neck, if you have nothing to eat, if your house is on fire, then you have a problem. Everything else is inconvenience. Life is inconvenient. Life is lumpy."

Sigmund Wollman

Up to this point, we have been looking at how the complete cycle of attitude fits together as well as the two main attitude paths that people follow (see the diagram at the end of chapter 7). Now it's time to consider some specific issues that can help us put our newfound understanding to work. In this chapter, we will take a closer look at the subject of frustration. Since the FRUSTRATION phase is where our attitude train jumps the track, we can benefit by preparing ourselves to handle frustration in the best possible manner.

THE NATURE OF FRUSTRATION

Webster's dictionary defines frustration as a "deep, chronic sense of insecurity arising from unresolved problems." This definition makes frustration sound like a severe psychological disorder requiring the advice and care of a physician. If your experiences are this severe, then I would encourage you to consult your doctor; however, for this book, a milder version of this definition should be sufficient. Let's define frustration simply as a sense of insecurity arising from unresolved problems. In this way, we can deal with the garden variety of frustrations ourselves and leave the really troublesome, chronic ones to doctors of psychiatry and medicine.

Armed with this definition, we can begin to investigate the nature of frustration. First, we know that frustration is universal: Everyone on earth has to deal with it. Like eating, breathing and sleeping, frustration is a natural part of living. Second, we know that frustration is inevitable. We cannot avoid it. Third, we know that frustration produces uncomfortable feelings for us, often leading to anger. Finally, and most importantly, we know that frustration is a product of the human mind. (When it grabs us and takes us for a ride, it is only because we have given our permission.)

Frustration is associated with experiences ranging from quickly forgotten nuisances, irritations and disappointments to heavy-duty, exasperating, constantly present aggravations. Minor irritations, like burning a piece of toast every once in a while, are easily dismissed. We can shrug these off most of the time. But if the irritations or problems continue, frustration can build into a much bigger, more difficult to resolve, emotional problem.

For example, the irritating actions of young children are

usually minor when examined individually, but they can add up rapidly to produce strong feelings of anxiety, stress and anger in everyone around them. Similarly, we know that when couples first fall in love, they often overlook minor conflicts and annoying behavior. Over time, however, frustrations can accumulate, leading to deep feelings of hurt or anger. Longer, sustained periods of frustration cause people to quit their jobs, divorce their spouses and abandon their life's dreams. In extreme cases, the cumulative effect of unresolved frustration can lead to deep-seated illness or perhaps even suicide.[1]

FRUSTRATION TOLERANCE LEVEL

Each of us has a "frustration tolerance level" that we have developed as a result of life's conditioning process. For most of us, the level is reasonably high, allowing us to deal with at least one source of stress. As long as the water in our frustration tank doesn't overflow, we can periodically drain the tank and experience relief. However, when frustrations rain down upon us regularly, or from multiple sources, or when the drain line is plugged, our tank can overflow, leaving us to deal with a flood of emotion.

As we have seen, frustration overflow can cause major problems with our attitude. The accumulation of sufficient irritants at work or in our relationships is what ultimately leads to the FRUSTRATION phase of our attitude cycle and its various subphases: shock, denial, fear, anger, justification and acceptance.

The flood of negative emotion presents us with the choice we have already reviewed at length: We can react constructively to the flood, or we can react destructively. In most cases, RECOMMITMENT is the constructive response, and it can help us counteract the negative emotional effects of

FRUSTRATION.

We will be even better prepared to defend our attitude if we can somehow prevent an attack of frustration in the first place, or eliminate the frustration once it occurs. This is the focus of this chapter. To head off frustration, or to eliminate it once it has begun, we have to understand what causes it. When we zero in on a cause, we can take action to neutralize it.

WHAT CAUSES FRUSTRATION?

Remember our definition? Frustration is "a sense of insecurity arising from unresolved problems." In our careers, an acute level of frustration overflow develops when we feel out of control — when too many unresolved problems pile up. This can happen quickly if the results we are getting do not measure up to our expectations or if our achievements are falling short of our goals.

Our inner being is designed to bring our actions into harmony with our controlling thoughts, similar to the way an autopilot tries to keep an airplane on course. Just like airplanes, we do not have total control over all of the things that affect us. Airplanes have to deal with foul weather and other airplanes flying around. Pilots can enter erroneous headings, and enemy forces can shoot destructive missiles. So even with the autopilot, planes can crash.

Planes occasionally crash, and so do people. Since we cannot stay in control at all times, we will experience periods of frustration. When we can get our achievements back up to where we want them to be, the frustration goes away. On the other hand, frustration that is allowed to linger and fester like an untreated wound often leads to the negative attitude cycle we have already discussed. Like an airplane out of control,

76

we crash.

In relationships, both at home and in the workplace, frustration develops primarily over unmet expectations. One person expects another person to behave or perform in a certain way, and when that doesn't happen, feelings of aggravation develop. We feel uncomfortable because we cannot get the other person to change or to act within our desired timeframe. This relates directly to our need to be in control. When we are in control, everything is fine. When we are out of control, we are frustrated.

RESPOND IN A POSITIVE WAY

At times, you may be in a position of wanting to keep the job you hold or wanting to maintain a relationship, but you are feeling very frustrated. You are feeling a need to relieve the pressure of the frustration pressure-cooker because it has paralyzed your effectiveness or your relationship. If this is where you are, you have recognized your frustration, and that is a major accomplishment. You know where you are in the attitude cycle, and now you can choose which path to take. (You will take the positive path, won't you?)

FIRST STEP

Your first step towards eliminating your frustration is to step back emotionally from the feelings of frustration. Since the wrong emotional response to frustration is the true enemy, we have to prevent our emotions from going awry. We must fight to stay in emotional control while we decide how to respond to the irritation(s). As we will see, irritation can stem from real or imagined sources. It is important to note that regardless of the source, we can choose to deal with frustration in a positive way. Whether we make the decision consciously or unconsciously, this is the choice we want to make.

SECOND STEP

Once we have made the decision to stay in control of our emotions and to constructively focus them, we can begin to identify the specific cause of our frustration. We can start with a series of questions:

What is irritating me? (See text box, next page.)
Why do I feel the way I do?
Is it because I'm dissatisfied with my own performance?
Is it because others are putting pressure on me?
Is there an obstacle in my way that someone can remove?
Is it because someone else hasn't done something that I wanted them to do?
Is it because someone won't act the way I want them to?
Is it because I need someone to relieve me for a while?
Is it because I'm in over my head and need some help?
Are my standards of performance too high and in need of adjustment?
Am I trying to be perfect in an imperfect world?
Am I expecting perfection from others?

These questions, and others like them, help us identify the things that are causing us to feel so uncomfortable. Patience, time and effort will usually lead us to some good answers. I try to be completely honest with myself, and it isn't too difficult because I don't have to share my feelings with others unless I deem it appropriate.

It's also important to look for more than one cause. Since the cause or causes may be subtle and hard to discern, it may help to write out the answers or to draw diagrams. It can also help to rank them numerically, by priority or by impact. With

---

TYPICAL IRRITANTS

Noises
    Babies or young children
    Ringing telephones
    Motorcycles and trucks
    People talking
    Boom boxes and car stereos
Traffic
Crowds
Family
Delays
Information overload
Insufficient information
Disagreements
Lack of cooperation
Rapid change
Work overload
Improper tools
Inadequate knowledge
Insufficient funds (money)
Interruptions
Car trouble

---

some answers in hand, we can proceed to another question.

THIRD STEP: IS IT LIVE, OR IS IT MEMOREX?

Several years ago, a television commercial featured the voice of an opera singer shattering a crystal goblet. The question raised by the announcer was, "Is it live, or is it Memorex?" The manufacturer was making the point that recordings on Memorex tape were just as real as the live performance. Or more to the point, that the listener wouldn't be able to tell the difference. In the same way that opera performances come in both live and recorded versions, the obstacles that cause frustration come in two varieties: real and imaginary. For each one of the causes we have identified, we need to ask ourselves, "Is this a real obstacle in front of me, or is this an imaginary obstacle?" Knowing the difference will enable us to choose the most effective response.

If the obstacle is real, then we can begin to work systematically to remove it. An example of a real obstacle might be a sudden surge in the number of customers you have to deal with or a deadline that got changed without negotiation. It might be as simple as the need for a new piece of equipment — one that works reliably. Perhaps someone else in the department really isn't pulling his or her weight. In a relationship, it might be the sudden realization that the other person is dishonest; or, you may recognize the existence of activities that make achievement of your personal goals impossible.

Each of these obstacles can be confronted in a physical sense. We can get help to deal with the customers. We can renegotiate the deadline. We can purchase or lease a new piece of equipment. We can remove the person who isn't pulling his or her weight. We can choose how to more effectively interact with a dishonest person. Finally, we can work around, or perhaps remove, any activities that are preventing us from achieving our goals.

If the obstacle is imaginary, then we will need to resolve the problem in our own mind if we are to remove it. Imaginary obstacles include personal feelings of inadequacy, a feeling that someone in the organization is out to get you when they really aren't, feeling pressured to achieve a goal that seems impossible, or feeling that you are all alone in your task. The common denominator in these imaginary obstacles is F.E.A.R.: False Evidence Appearing Real.

We want everything to go well, but we are unable to clearly see the future. Because we are fearful, we mentally project worst-case scenarios. When this is done vividly enough, or often enough, these scenarios grow more powerful. Eventually, the negative scenes drown out the positive ones. Then, our most feared case becomes the outcome we truly expect to see.

Let's look at an example.

Dinah Nicholson is a top-producing sales representative for a national financial services firm. She was asked to respond to the phrase, "If I knew then what I know now... " This is what she wrote:

"I would have been better prepared for those brick walls you keep coming up against in the beginning. I call them 'learning walls' or 'psychological walls.' Like the wall you hit when you've worked hard, done everything exactly right and all of sudden, you get total rejection. The thing I learned about walls was that each time I hit one, there was something — usually an attitude — that I had to change. Fear of failure, fear of success, fear of not being good enough. That first year, all our personal weaknesses come out, and we have to say, 'Okay, I'm not perfect. What can I change? What can't I — or won't I — change?' The most successful reps I know are the ones who have faced those walls, asked — and answered — those hard questions and adjusted their attitudes accordingly."[2]

Remember, "Nothing is to be feared. It is only to be understood." As Dinah figured out, it was the way she was responding to the stimulus that needed changing, not the stimulus itself. She had to adjust her thinking. She had to understand the fear and decide consciously that it was false evidence. With that understanding, she was in a position to move forward and become one of the company's top representatives. Note, also, that she decided to change herself — her own attitude — rather than trying to get the world around her to change.

Even when the concerns we face are imaginary, most of us will argue that the obstacles are real. We know, intuitively, that dragons are imaginary and that we shouldn't be afraid of them. So, we will do everything we can to create a REAL obstacle — even if this means lying to ourselves — and rationalizing that an imaginary obstacle is real. To make sure that we are actually facing a REAL obstacle, we should seek confirmation from someone else or by doing some research. If we can prove the obstacle is real, then we can work to remove it.

FOURTH STEP - THE CRITICAL FACTOR

Once you have clearly identified what is causing your frustration, ask yourself, "Would my frustration go away if *this* cause did not exist?" If the answer is no, you need to think more about what is causing the problem because you have not yet identified the root cause.[3] When you can answer yes, ask yourself, "What can *I* do to eliminate the cause?" Or, "What *must* I do to eliminate the cause?"

If you are having trouble digging out the root cause of the problem on your own, then seek out your boss or others in your company who are older and wiser. Present your problem in a positive, solution-seeking way. Try to get a variety of opinions and possible solutions, but be careful to avoid sharing your frustrations with too many people. Numerous well-meaning employees have been forced to change jobs because of the negative ways they went about seeking change.

When you have some answers in hand, work to eliminate the critical factor causing your frustration. You can use one or more of the following steps:

1. Eliminate it yourself, if you can. Make a behavioral change, or change the way you think about something. (See chapter 6 and the RECOMMITMENT Phase.) Take action to fix the equipment, or buy the equipment you need to get the job done. Move things around to prevent bottlenecks. Take a course in computer programming, time management or shorthand. Work harder, longer or smarter — but get the obstacle(s) behind you.

2. If you can't eliminate it by yourself, can someone else do it for you? Whose help do you need? Can your boss remove it for you? Your business partner? A co-worker? Another team member? Your spouse? Your children? Prepare a mutually beneficial proposal, then talk with them. Negotiate a solution, if possible, but at least get the problem on the table, and ask for their help. Usually a partial solution is better than none at all. And generally speaking, the more heads, the better, when you are looking for alternative solutions. (Caution: Be careful not to accuse, or otherwise offend, the person whose help you are seeking.)

3. Get some outside, professional advice. This can help you invent a solution or a creative way to approach and solve the problem.

4. Once you have eliminated the cause of your frustration, make a quick pit stop in the RECOMMITMENT area, then head back out to the EXCITEMENT track.

Confronting your frustration and anger by taking the kind

of constructive action just described is a crucial step. It is often difficult to approach a boss, a partner, a spouse, a customer or a child, especially when they are a big part of the problem. Sometimes, it takes determination and tenacity, but *it has to be done.* Remember, however, to **confront in a constructive manner.** I will address this issue in more detail in the next few chapters.

WRONG AND RIGHT RESPONSES

One of the wrong ways to handle our frustration is to mishandle the anger we are feeling. It is a mistake to camouflage our anger by faking harmony, remaining silent or covering up with gooey sweetness. It is also unwise to suppress your anger and allow your frustrations to accumulate in an unresolved anger tank. The energy from these suppressed feelings can manifest itself in other forms, such as guilt, obesity, insomnia, psychosomatic illnesses, backaches, dermatological conditions, headaches, gastrointestinal symptoms and ulcers — even sexual problems and fatigue.[4]

We also know it is almost always a mistake to be overtly angry. Unless you have an alterior motive, public criticism is the wrong kind of confrontation for anyone to make. It is also a mistake to be a closet critic — to harbor an undertone of anger, hostility and negativism. Neither one of these approaches will get you promoted, and they may even get you fired without explanation.

I once knew a promising young executive who was confident that he was right and the company was wrong. He made the mistake of telling several people high up in the company how he felt. A couple of months later, they offered him a choice between leaving or being put out to pasture where his opinions wouldn't matter anymore. He chose to leave. So even if he was right, he lost out on a promising career because he didn't reveal his anger in a positive, constructive, solution-oriented manner.

There is an ideal way to handle anger, and a very mature person will attempt to handle it in this way. It involves a combination of things. First, he doesn't save up anger stamps, and because of this, he has dealt with all of the previous anger in his life and his unresolved anger tank is empty. He doesn't hold anger inside where it can be destructive to himself, either.

Second, his response to irritating factors is by choice rather than by reaction. It is a controlled, somewhat delayed response.

Third, he is principle driven. This means that he is willing to get visibly angry, but only when injustices are done or other people's lives are at stake.

And fourth, his anger leads to positive action. He constructively dissipates his anger in a way that harms others the least yet leads to positive results.[5] Very few of us will ever approach this ideal, but at least we have something to work toward.

PREVENTING FRUSTRATION

As we have noted several times, frustration is inevitable. We cannot completely prevent it. Just like ants at a picnic, it is always present, even in the positive side of the cycle. But we can take steps to prevent it from occurring too often, and we can reduce the number of things that cause us to have feelings of frustration.

In my experience, the people who make quantum leaps in reducing the amount of overall frustration in their lives are the ones who work hardest at time management. Over a period of time — sometimes weeks, sometimes years — they somehow determine what really matters in their life. They sort through their basic beliefs and values and goals. Then, they spend their time working at activities that support those beliefs, values and goals. This focus allows them to minimize the non-meaningful events in their lives, thus increasing the feeling of satisfaction and decreasing the frustration associated with waste and wheel-spinning.

Another thing we can do is work at increasing our frustration-tolerance level. We can stop trying to be a perfectionist, if that is our calling. We can let more things go by without criticism or complaint. We can try to better determine what is really important and worth being concerned about. These suggestions are often grouped under the heading "Keeping Things in Proper Perspective." If your standards are too high, or your reference points are too specific, you may be setting yourself up for a lot of extra frustration in your life. I'm not suggesting that you lower all of your standards, just the ones that won't make a critical difference in your life. We can pursue excellence without demanding perfection at every turn.

Parents can help their children become more successful as adults if they will work to increase the child's frustration-tolerance level. When it is clear that a child is in the FRUS-TRATION phase, then our responsibility is to coach them into, and then through, the RECOMMITMENT phase. In this way, we can show them how to successfully and systematically work through the obstacles in their lives.

Supervisors can help their associates by anticipating frustrating events or changes and helping their employees cope with the event or the transition. We can also coach our associates into and through the RECOMMITMENT phase. I'll have more on this later.

REOCCURRING FRUSTRATION

If our frustration keeps reoccurring, it is even more important to make a thorough analysis of the cause of the irritation. If we have been attacking the wrong cause, then the frustration will keep returning. We may also be facing multiple causes at the same time, which can cloud our ability to clearly see the root cause or causes. It might be beneficial to work with someone skilled in cause-effect analysis, or perhaps a trained counselor, if this is what you are facing.

As we know, the biggest problem with frustration is the negative consequences that can emanate from the emotional feelings of shock, denial, fear and anger. With prolonged frustration, we will build up a considerable amount of hostility and indignation. If we simply reject these feelings over a long period of time, our unconscious mind will take control and totally eliminate the feeling part of the process. When we switch our emotional responder to "autopilot" in this fashion, the anger can be manifested in many different forms. We may not feel anything, or we might simply feel numb, hurt, disappointed, irritated or annoyed. Anger that is repressed in this fashion will ultimately seek expression in some sort of aggressive, defensive or destructive manner against either ourselves or others. So it is important to get some help and work towards an effective solution.

SUPPRESSED (MUTED) FRUSTRATION

You may be one of the many people who is trapped in a career or relationship that does not utilize your talents to the fullest. You may have unknowingly placed yourself within a comfort zone where you are able to tolerate the level of frustration you experience. If this describes your situation, then you may find it very hard to maintain yourself in an EXCITE-MENT phase because you aren't working towards much of a dream. My best advice to you would be to think about what your dreams really are and to begin working towards them. As Seneca, the Greek philosopher, noted, "When a man does not know what harbor he's making for, no wind is the right wind."

Our goals must be clear. This may mean changing careers, making new friends, dropping long-cherished beliefs or even getting a divorce. When a car proves itself to be a lemon, it's time to get a new one.

OVERCOMING FRUSTRATION

All of us have experienced some degree of adversity in our lives, and all of us have overcome it with a variety of achievements along the way. The degree to which we recognize those achievements and give ourselves credit for our ability to overcome adversity will play a large part in defining the level of self-confidence we will be able to call upon when we have to deal with the next set of frustrating experiences in our life. Keep a file or a list of the achievements and successful experiences in your life, and refer to it periodically as a reminder that you can succeed.

RECOGNIZING YOUR OWN STRENGTHS

Think back over your life at this point, and make a note of some of the challenges you have faced and successfully overcome. Write your strengths on the Personal Assets Form in this chapter. This exercise will help you realize that you *do* have the ability to deal with frustration successfully. It will help you discover where and how you have successfully dealt with frustration before.

You might also test the concepts in this book as you go along. When you have improved your ability to deal with frustration, you will be ready to move on to more challenging assignments, higher goals and greater fulfillment. You will be on your way to becoming a Super Achiever.

[1]Dwight Carlson, M.D., **Overcoming Hurts & Anger** (Harvest House Publishers, 1981), p. 27.
[2]**Waddell & Reed World**, Vol 35, No. 2, February, 1995.
[3]The root cause is the cause from which all other causes stem. The problem you are facing might be attributable to many different causes, but there is probably only one cause that, in turn, causes all of the other causes. You need to keep digging until you find the root.
[4]Carlson, p. 26.
[5]Ibid., 60-61.

PERSONAL ASSETS FORM

A challenge I successfully faced and overcame was:

_____

_____

I dealt with the FRUSTRATION phase of this challenge by:

_____

_____

The specific strengths and personal abilities I showed in doing so were:

_____

_____

Chapter 10

Working For, or With, Someone Else

"Attitude is the first quality that marks the successful man. If he has a positive attitude and is a positive thinker, who likes challenges and difficult situations, then he has half his success achieved. On the other hand, if he is a negative thinker who is narrow-minded and refuses to accept new ideas and has a defeatist attitude, he hasn't got a chance."

Lowell Peacock

$\mathbf{A}$t this point in our journey, we should be well acquainted with the four phases of attitude, as well as the two cycles: positive and negative. We also have a better understanding of frustration and how to avoid some of it. The next logical step is to apply this knowledge to our work.

This chapter is about how to work with your supervisor or business partner. Although many of the concepts can be used to improve our marriages, our relationships with our children and the rest of our lives, this chapter is mainly about work. In the next chapter, we will consider things from the supervisor's point of view, but this one is devoted to the employee.

To begin this leg of our journey, it will be helpful to digress into a bit of philosophy. In order for any of us to be able to use the four-phases concept well, we must have the right frame of mind to begin with — the right philosophy about life and work. As the great psychologist, William James, said, "It is *our* attitude *at the beginning* of a difficult undertaking which, more than anything else, will determine its successful outcome."

It is our **attitude**.

It is *our* attitude.

It is our attitude *at the beginning*.

What should our attitude be at the beginning of a career, a long-term project or a relationship? If everyone came to the table with a feeling of positive expectancy, that is, expecting things to go well, and then maintained that feeling at all times, even in the face of demanding obstacles, all would be well. As we already know, most of us have difficulty doing that on a regular basis, and that is what this book is all about.

There are a few things that we, as employees, as spouses or as parents, can bring to the situation which will make it easier to adapt the four phases for our benefit. This may sound a little bit like a lecture at times, and if it does, I apologize. But please understand that tall buildings need firm foundations, big trees need deep roots and human beings need solid attitudinal support on which to build a magnificent life. So, whether you work *for* somebody else or *with* somebody else, or when you *live* with somebody else, here are four key success factors you can bring with you as a gift for all concerned.

KEYS TO SUCCESS

First, we have to **accept and take responsibility for our *own* attitude, our *own* job and our *own* life.** Getting our job done is not our employer's responsibility, it is ours. At home, or in a partnership, this means taking responsibility for more than half of the work. I say more than half, because if both parties approach life from this point of view, neither one will ever have anything to complain about. How can you complain when the other party is doing more than his or her share of the work?

When we work for somebody else, we have accepted a contract. We have taken on the responsibility of working towards that employer's goals, whatever they may be. The employer has some responsibility toward us, like paying us as agreed and following the laws of the land, but not necessarily as much responsibility as we have in return. We are expected to live up to the terms of the contract, and that generally means doing whatever we are assigned to do.

When we live with somebody, in a marriage, for example, we have accepted a similar responsibility, only now it is a shared and equal responsibility. Each person has a mutual responsibility to each other because you both have goals that should be considered.

When we work with somebody else, in a partnership, for example, it is like living with somebody. Each party has a responsibility to the other, and both have goals that need to be recognized.

So, as Theodore Roosevelt said, "Whenever you are asked if you can do a job, tell 'em, 'Certainly I can!' Then get busy and find out how to do it."

Second, **come to work with a positive, expectant attitude.** Drop life's petty troubles off at the city dump. Leave

93

them behind. Remember that you will be passing the dump again tomorrow, and let that wash away any troubles that crop up during the day. Add a symbolic trash can at work to handle any negatives that just won't wait for tomorrow's drop-off. Be happy, and expect others to be that way. Be a lightning rod of good cheer and optimism. Radiate good will and faith in a better, brighter future — even when things look bleak.

> What good did it do to be grouchy today? Did your surliness drive any trouble away?
> Did you cover more ground than you usually do because of the grouch you carried with you?
> If not, what's the use of a grouch or a frown if it won't smooth a path or a grim trouble drown?
> If it doesn't assist you, it isn't worthwhile. Your work may be hard, but just do it — and smile.

> Anonymous[1]

As you look at the kinds of people you like to be around, my guess is you're much like me. I gravitate towards people who have a handle on dealing with difficult circumstances. They always seem to see the positive in everything. They see the calm after the storm, the gold at the end of the rainbow and the silver lining in the dark cloud. I find myself drawn to people with this outlook on life, which leads me to a blinding flash of common sense: You can be just like that. It's your choice.

Third, **solve problems, don't fix blame.** It is far better to try and fix a problem than it is to spend all of your time fixing blame on someone else. Most of the time, the blame belongs on the shoulders of more than one person, anyway. Seldom is one person solely responsible for a situation.

One of the most common components of the blame game is asking questions. We are always asking, "Why?" Why do we do things this way? Why doesn't the boss change this? Why doesn't the company change that? Why does it have to be this difficult? Some of this questioning is good, because without such questions, nothing would ever change for the better. But when the tone becomes negative and cynical, questions cease to be good. *We cross the line when we expect others to be responsible for the changes we want.*

Take the first question in the previous paragraph as an example. "Why do we do things this way?" This question can be asked in several ways. When asked in a constructive way, it becomes the prelude to a solution. For example, if my intent in asking the question is to seek improved ways of doing things, and I ask it with positive expectancy, then anyone who is listening will be motivated to help me understand the current approach. Perhaps a good idea or a new approach will surface during the discussion.

On the other hand, the same question can be asked in a condescending, negative, sarcastic way. This tone instantly conjures up a defensive, protectionist response in anyone who feels responsible for the situation being questioned. In asking the question in this fashion, it is quite obvious that *the questioner is NOT taking any responsibility* for the way things are done. This leads to a harmful, confrontational discussion instead of a productive, contributional one.

The second, third and fourth questions from the paragraph above are even more obvious in their negative intent. They immediately imply that the boss and the company or life in general is to blame for the situation and that only those entities can do anything about it.

It is so easy to fall into the trap of blaming others for the problems we face. We blame the boss, blame the company, blame the government, blame our parents, blame our children, blame our circumstances — and we do it *without even realizing* we are doing it. Yet it is our choice. Let's make it a point to *let others play the blame game without us*. The following story illustrates why this is important.

It was a miserably hot and humid day. With several other bus drivers out sick, it had become especially long for the driver of a particular city bus. As the bus headed along the boulevard, a young woman passenger, apparently very frustrated about something, let loose with a string of unforgettable, mostly undesirable words. The bus driver, who watched the scene unfold in the overhead mirror, could sense that all of the other passengers were very embarrassed by the string of profanity.

A short while later, the angry passenger pulled the string to sound the buzzer, then came forward to the front door. As she headed down the steps, the bus driver calmly said, "Madam, I believe you are leaving something behind."

Turning quickly, she snapped, "Oh, and what is that?"

"A very bad impression," the bus driver responded.[2]

The last of my four suggestions is to **get in the habit of responding in the positive direction of the cycle** when we find ourselves at the pivotal point in a FRUSTRATION phase. This is an up-front, at-the-beginning decision. We are seldom prepared mentally, in advance, for the hard work and the frustration we will experience on the job, but having read this book, we have no more excuses!

Nicolo Paganini had the right habit. He was a violinist in the 19th century, well known for his great showmanship and quick sense of humor. At a memorable concert in Italy, he was performing before a packed house with a full orchestra behind him. The fluidity of his technique was incredible, and the sounds from his violin showed his amazing versatility as he moved from one mood to another. His audience clearly loved him.

Toward the end of his concert, Paganini was astounding his audience with an unbelievable composition when a string on his violin snapped loose. With the string hanging limply from his instrument, Paganini frowned briefly. He shook his head and continued to play, improvising beautifully. Moments later, to everyone's astonishment, a second string broke. And shortly thereafter, a third. In what might have been the original slapstick comedy, Paganini stood there with three strings dangling from his Stradivarius. *But instead of quitting and leaving the stage, Paganini calmly stood his ground, completing the difficult number as best he could on his one remaining string.* We would all do well to emulate Nicolo Paganini when the strings of our lives go haywire.[3]

Ask yourself, "What am I going to do about it? I understand that I will have some degree of difficulty in all areas of my life. That's normal. I can't change it. I will be subject to their negative impact. I do have the right to make choices about my response to those changes."

Dr. Steven Covey, in his book **The Seven Habits of Highly Successful People**, says habit one is "Be Proactive." When I take a proactive stance with the anger I feel, my attitude has a good chance of standing tall.

HOW THE FOUR PHASES CAN HELP - GENERALLY

Employers expect us to get the job done and, just as importantly, to get it done without griping. Part of our paycheck is compensating us for the difficulty we face. So first, we need to recognize that we are getting paid to face each difficulty. Second, we need to concentrate on developing positive responses to the inevitable difficulties as they arrive.

The four-phases concept helps us recognize when it is time to take charge and develop these responses.

Robert Schuller, author of **Tough Times Don't Last, But Tough People Do**, once said, "It's all important that you develop a positive attitude toward problems. Let me suggest four attitudinal philosophies toward problems. Two are positive, and two are negative. You have four choices when you run into any problem. Your first choice is to resent it. Your second choice is simply to consent to it. Your third choice is to invent a solution. And your fourth possibility is to prevent the problem from getting worse and from coming back at you later."

I like his third suggestion the best: invent a solution. If life gives you a choice between chocolate and vanilla, and you don't like either one, make strawberry. When you face problems, frustrations or challenges, ask yourself, "What opportunity do I have right now? How can I respond in a positive, inventive, solution-oriented way? How can I overcome this frustration and be a winner?" (Note the emphasis in each question on the word I. Remember, you are the only one who can do something about the problem.)

You might still be thinking, "Even if I'm absolutely, positively convinced I am not to blame?" Yes! Even when I'm absolutely certain that it's a problem with the company, the system or the other person in the relationship, I still have to assume responsibility, then take positive action to make things change. That might mean negotiation, discussion, some other action on my part or simply making do with what I have until things change. This philosophy is summed up well in the following quote from an anonymous source:

"When I was young and free and my imagination had no limits, I dreamed of changing the world. As I grew older and wiser, I discovered the world would not change, so I shortened my sights somewhat and decided to change only my country. But it, too, seemed immovable. As I grew into my twilight years, in one last, desperate attempt, I settled for changing only my family, those closest to me, but alas, they would have none of it. And now, as I lie on my deathbed, I suddenly realize: If I had only changed myself first, then, by example, I might have changed my family. From their inspiration and encouragement, I would then have been able to better my country, and, who knows, I may have even changed the world."

SPECIFIC PROBLEMS AND THE FOUR PHASES

What does the four-phases concept tell us, as an employee, that we should do? It tells us to expect problems and even to welcome them, because that is how we make progress up the ladder. It also tells us to respond in a positive, constructive way when we encounter FRUSTRATION. This means we should take personal responsibility for finding a solution to the problem, whatever it may be and regardless of who might be worthy of blame. As I noted above, it's critical to avoid playing the blame game. Also, as my good friend Bob Sabino says, "Wise is the person who sees opportunity in difficulty. Rich is the one who makes something beneficial out of difficulty."

If the problem is imaginary, and the frustration is only being experienced because of the way we are thinking, we simply need to recommit to our original dream and dig back in. If the problem is real, and our anger is legitimate, then we should begin to look for creative, inventive solutions to the problem. There is an age-old, four-step, common-sense process that helps with this. It's also good to involve our mentor or red-flag partner in the process, too.

Step one is to crystallize the problem by asking, "What is the problem?" While this question sounds simple, this step may be the hardest because we must choose the right problem to work on. Coming up with a solution to the wrong problem seldom gets us where we want to go.

The window frame through which we view the problem also determines what we will see when we go looking for solutions, so spend a lot of time getting the answer to this first question. How? By approaching it from a variety of angles and looking beyond the obvious. It helps to rephrase and clarify, clarify, clarify. It also helps to rephrase and simplify, simplify, simplify. Keep asking yourself, "What is the problem?"

Step two asks, "What causes this problem to exist?" Once again, we need to think carefully in order to dig out the root cause. Addressing the wrong cause will not solve our problem any more than addressing the wrong problem will. We may need to sort through many apparent causes for the problem and then narrow it down to one by asking what is causing all of the various causes to appear? A popular method of doing this is to ask "Why?" five times. Each time you ask the question, you are digging further down towards the root.

Step three asks, "What are all the ways I could solve this problem?" Since we know exactly what the problem is, and what is causing it, it should be a simple matter of listing various ways to address or eliminate the cause. At times, we may require some creative, unique or special solutions, so we need to keep an open mind — and ask other people for ideas!

Step four is to select a solution from the options listed in the previous step. Hopefully, you can simply choose the best solution and implement it; however, you may not be able to choose the best solution from your list if it requires resources you don't have or approval you cannot get. On the other hand, you may be able to combine several options and create an even better solution. The most important factor is to select at least one, then *TAKE ACTION!*

With a long list of different solutions, we will have a better chance of getting rid of the problem. Few problems are truly resolved with just one fix. And, by the way, working on a long list will give us many successes and job security, too.

WHICH PROBLEMS GET ADDRESSED?

A good friend of mine told me about the following learning experience:

"One of my most revealing insights as a manager was when I realized that problems need to be prioritized and that some might never be addressed. Frustrated over the lack of efficiency in my department, I submitted a request for funds to purchase a piece of equipment that could make some parts we used regularly. I strongly believed it would help my department be more professional and productive. In denying the request, my boss wrote back that he had a limited amount of money to spend, and he had to choose among many good ideas. I learned that when resources are limited, problem resolution is limited, too. I had to find another solution for my frustration. In this case, it was continuing to purchase the needed parts instead of making them."

Even when the resources are available to take care of a recognized problem, there may not be any pressure to act. Other problems may be taking priority, or there may not be enough incentive for action.

As employees, we can help our employers and supervisors recognize problems, we can help bring pressure to act on them and we can help provide the necessary manpower and resources to effect a solution.

At the same time, we must be willing to accept our employer's choice of solution, even if it isn't the one we would choose. Having a good solution to a real problem within our grasp, and then not being able to implement our chosen solution because of situations beyond our control, can be the most frustrating situation of all. But like Paganini, we need to keep playing — on whatever strings are available to us — until we can take time to repair the violin. Such a situation might result in additional frustration and lead to yet another round of problem-solving.

CONFRONTING PROBLEMS

So far, we've seen that it is important to approach our lives with the right attitude, and that we must actually take responsibility for solving the problems we encounter. We've also seen how to approach those problems and select a proposed solution. What do we do next? When we can implement our solution without the help of other people, then the answer is obvious. We implement it, quickly RECOMMIT to our dreams and move back into EXCITEMENT.

To employees or partners in marriage or business, problems are usually not that simple. We may need approval to implement our plan. Or perhaps the boss, our partner, our spouse or our customer has control over the root cause of our problem. They may be doing something that is irritating us, or they may not be doing something we feel they should be doing. Regardless of the specifics, we will need to confront the other party. Here is an example, as related to me by George Thompson.

"I was doing some work at home when my 2-year-old son began to crawl up on my desk. He quickly became a real source of frustration. Shock, denial and fear quickly passed into anger. In some situations, all four subphases seem to just melt into one, and I just blow up. My temper became short, and I found myself mentally blaming my wife for having left the child at home with me while she ran some errands. How dare she place her priorities over mine? I also felt anger toward my 13-year-old son, who was just sitting there letting it all happen. He was aware of my need to concentrate, and he was aware of the high priority my work had become — yet he did nothing. It was time for a confrontation.

"Adrenaline was pumping through my veins. My first instinct was to get very angry — to scream and yell and order both of them around. Instead, I deliberately stepped back emotionally and took control of my own feelings first. The problem was clear. The cause of my frustration was clear. The solutions were also clear. Either I could stop work, or my 13-year-old son could take the 2 year old away. As calmly as I could under the circumstances, I presented these alternatives to my 13 year old. Good son that he is, he rose to the occasion and took responsibility for the 2 year old. The best possible solution was in place. With the source of my frustration removed, I was able to recommit to the goal of finishing my work and move back into the happy excitement of production."

Confrontation does not have to be difficult. It does not have to be negative. It does not have to be emotional. Unfortunately, many times it is. To confront is to challenge the other party, and when challenged, people have a physiological response that is automatic and chemically driven. Our body prepares us for fight or flight. The degree to which we respond depends on how the challenge presents itself. If we feel threatened, we respond angrily and defensively. When we control our emotions and do not feel threatened, we can then more calmly assess our alternatives.

When we are frustrated, and other people are holding the key to freedom from that frustration, we owe it to ourselves to confront them. To the extent that we can, we need to present our case with tact and skill.

Human relations skills are critical for everyone. This is especially true if we are parents because we are modelling the coping skills our child will be emulating later in life. Many books have been written on this subject, and it is far too broad to deal with in these pages, but we need to be absolutely clear on one point: *Confrontation is an essential tool for the successful management of frustration in our lives.* Failing to confront issues important to you is taking the easy way out emotionally. This often results in the problem never being resolved. At some level, your turmoil will persist indefinitely, which is what typically happens with destructively handled anger. Over a lifetime, a person who repeatedly handles anger-producing situations in this way will build up a tremendous amount of hurt and troubled relationships. Reversal of the problem at that point is extremely difficult, so it is far better to curtail it early on.

Three pieces of advice may help you utilize the tool of confrontation effectively.

First and foremost, you must set aside any fear of being put down for confronting an issue important to you. If something is causing frustration overflow in our life, then it is our duty to act. Expressing anger in a constructive way will never damage a worthwhile relationship. It simply indicates that you care enough about the person to work out the problems in the relationship, no matter how painful the issue or process might be. A relationship destroyed from a constructive attempt at confrontation was probably a weak relationship to begin with.[4]

Second, approach every confrontation knowing that the other person might be right. In some cases, it is wise to be very open minded on this point (such as when dealing with your boss). In others, you need only leave a crack in the door (such as when dealing with your children) but never close it completely.

Third, try to confront in private, unless others have observed the conflict or are involved themselves, in which case you may need to bring the issue out in public. Another reason to go public is if the person you need to confront refuses to deal with you in private. Whenever possible, public confrontation should be used selectively and as a last resort.

SPECIFIC SITUATIONS

Now, let's talk specifically about some of the most common attitudinal situations we face when working with or living with others, and how the four-phases concept can help. In all of the examples that follow, you will notice that a fundamental aspect of getting your attitude under control is making sure that the other person doesn't lose control of his or hers in the process.

Managing conflict constructively. We all know that a conflict free-relationship just isn't possible. We can fool ourselves for a while, trying to ignore the variety of minor hurts and disappointments, but even the best of friends will disagree from time to time. These disagreements can quickly become the kind of frustration that takes us out of EXCITEMENT. How should we react when this happens? How should we handle it?

First, it's critical to avoid the blame game. When we experience conflict and frustration, it's quite natural to begin with an accusation. We often say things like, "You never do the work when you're supposed to," or "You haven't done anything I've asked you to do." These direct frontal assaults immediately put the other person on the defensive and often increase the level of conflict and tension instead of lowering it. They are seen as judgmental, critical attacks, and they leave little room for the other person to maneuver.

If attacking the other person isn't going to help us get the result we want, then we should let them attack us, right? Sorry, that isn't the right answer, either. The best approach is to try to keep things as conflict free as possible. We don't want to increase the other person's frustration.

What we want to do first is make the other person receptive to our position. Often, the best technique is simply to share our feelings with statements like, "I feel uncomfortable when work doesn't get done on time," or "I feel like I'm the one who has to do all the work around here." Statements like these do not directly criticize the other person, and they leave room for him or her to offer an explanation, an apology, a promise of changed behavior or an explanation of his or her true feelings.

It is hard for someone to argue about how another person feels, and in a mutually supportive relationship (or when trying to build one), such statements allow the other person to understand how you feel without feeling threatened personally. Many times, the other person will begin to probe for the cause of those feelings. If not, he or she will usually be open to further discussion aimed at resolving them. So if you can, try to keep your own emotions under control while still expressing your feelings and moving toward an objective, conflict-free discussion about how to improve things.

Problems with a co-worker: When we experience problems with our boss, we usually assume some degree of respect for the position the boss holds, and we humble ourselves somewhat. With a co-worker, we may not feel that humility is required. As a consequence, we tend to approach many problems with co-workers with an attitude of arrogance or a feeling of superiority. If we can guard against this tendency, and instead decide that we are both on equal ground, then we can approach the problem we are facing with control and objectivity. With this foundation, the technique for resolving the problem is much the same as it is with a boss — expressing your feelings without assigning blame, then asking for help in finding a mutually acceptable solution.

An old fable tells the story of a young lion and a cougar. Thirsty, the animals arrived at their usual watering hole at the same time. Out of false pride, they began to argue about who should satisfy his thirst first. The argument became heated, and each decided he would rather die than give up the privilege of being first. As they stubbornly confronted each other, their emotions turned to rage. But before they could consummate their vicious intentions, they were interrupted by sounds from above. Looking up, they saw a flock of vultures circling overhead, waiting for the loser to fall. Quietly, the two beasts turned and walked away. The thought of being devoured was all they needed to end their quarrel.

When co-workers are in conflict, nobody wins. Both are in FRUSTRATION, and both devote emotional energy to the battle. While it might sound trite, the solution is usually to shake hands, recommit to mutual goals and get EXCITED again.

You want something to change. As society continues to grow, one thing that seems to grow with it is the number of rules and policies we must obey. These rules and policies cause frequent frustration because they were designed to take care of specific conditions, yet many circumstances simply don't seem to match those conditions. For whatever reason, we feel that our situation should be recognized as an exception, or we feel that the rule, policy, regulation or restriction should be changed.

Let's assume you are right. The rule should be changed, and you've got lots of evidence and the support of all your friends or co-workers. It's now time to approach the boss. What do you do to get your way?

A fundamental tenet of leadership is to let the other person save face. One of the best ways of doing this is by humbling yourself. So if you want to propose change, start by asking the other person to help you. By saying you need help, you are taking a humble, submissive posture rather than a dominant, critical one. Virtually everyone likes to feel appreciated, and asking for help is one way of saying that you respect the other person, that you think he or she is really smart.

From this starting point, you can explain the problem you are having and suggest that the best solution is to change the policy. It helps to do your homework on the problem and to know the root cause. If you can show how the change will benefit the other person, too, then you've got an even better shot at success. As long as you present your problem and ask for help instead of attacking the policy and demanding change, you've got a good chance.

Getting something you want. A very common source of frustration in our lives, at work and at home is the feeling that if I just had one of those newfangled gadgets, then life would be really rosy and peachy-keen. Or perhaps you are feeling overloaded, and you have convinced yourself that a faster new computer would enable you to get everything done on time. When we can't get what we want right away, as in the case when a boss must approve the purchase or a spouse must agree to the expense, then we feel out of control and frustrated.

It's time to take a short course in negotiating. And here it is.

Start by identifying what you want, and then ask the other person what they want. Get all of the various issues on the table: what things cost, what will and won't work, what solutions they might propose. Then reach for compromise. How can you both get what you want?

The four-phases concept doesn't offer any specific help with this issue, but it does remind us that both parties have attitudes, and both experience periods of EXCITEMENT and FRUSTRATION. In a negotiation, too much FRUSTRATION with the process usually causes one of the parties to go LOOKING for another, less frustrating deal. So work hard at keeping yourself and your negotiating partner out of FRUSTRATION.

Traps, and how to get out of them. A fairly common attitudinal trap involves the family business. While many family businesses work out well for everyone involved, there are some that do not. If you are in a family business, you may feel trapped. You may feel like there's no way up, no way out and that you have no control over your situation. If this applies to you, you may simply have to make the best of a bad situation. If you want to stay in the business, your choices may be quite limited. Perhaps the best advice I can give you is to find a niche where you can excel, either inside or outside of the business, in a hobby or a project of some sort. This will give you something to commit to and get excited about. When you find your attitude slipping, you can recommit to these other dreams. Success in one part of our life can give us new strength to resolve frustration in another.

In other situations, it may be of benefit to work on an objective analysis of your situation. Do you really have to stay in the family business? What would happen if you left? To you? To your family? To the business? It may be time to dream a dream of your own instead of dreaming the family's dream. If so, you can create a plan of action based on your dreams, and then act upon it. It may require several contingency plans, or it may require biding your time. If biding your time is the only solution, then make the best of it by accepting the frustrating aspect of things and not letting them get to you.

This same advice would apply to those who are trapped in a dead-end job, as well as to those poor souls who are lost somewhere in a bureaucratic nightmare. As author Robert Walker once wrote, "Instead of weeping when a tragedy occurs in a songbird's life, it sings away its grief. I believe we could well follow the pattern of our feathered friends."

A long time ago, Charles Dickens wrote about a man in prison. Locked in a dungeon of despair and hopelessness, this captive longed for freedom. After many years, his day of liberation arrived. His captors led him from his gloomy cell out into the bright and beautiful world. Gazing for only a moment into the sunlight, he turned and walked back to his cell. Confinement had become so comfortable that the thought of freedom was overwhelming. Chains and darkness were his security.

Not unlike that prisoner, each of us has the opportunity to break free of the chains that bind us. Unfortunately, many of us have become secure in the rut of our negative thinking, so secure that the thought of change is frightening. Yet freedom comes only to those who are willing to trade away the security of imprisonment.[5]

In yet another prison, the captain gave the condemned man a choice. He could have death by firing squad, or he could walk through the green door, taking his chances with whatever he found behind it. Fearing all kind of evil behind the door, the man hesitated only briefly before choosing the firing squad.

As he was being led away to face death, the captain turned to one of his jailers, and said, "You see how it is with men. Always they choose the certain over the uncertain." The jailer then asked, "What lies behind the green door?" The captain replied, "Freedom. But I've only known a few who were brave enough to take it."

WHERE DOES AN EMPLOYEE GO FROM HERE?

This question reminds me of two famous stories about making your way through the intricacies of life. One of them is **Through a Looking Glass**, perhaps better known as **Alice in Wonderland**. At one point in her story, Alice is talking with the Cheshire Cat, and she asks him, "Which way do I go from here?" The cat replies, "It all depends on where you want to go." Alice responds, "It doesn't matter where." The cat retorts, "Then it doesn't matter which way you go."

How about you? Do you know where you want to go? Do you have a dream? Are you following the right path? Or are you wandering aimlessly through life?

The other famous story is about a young girl named Dorothy who somehow ends up in a strange land, far away from home. Undaunted, Dorothy dreams of going home to Kansas, and with the help of three unlikely heroes, she cycles in and out of EXCITEMENT and FRUSTRATION on her way to the Land of Oz. There, she hopes to find the great wizard, the boss man of Oz — the man with the plan — the man who can make her dream come true.

In the end, of course, Dorothy finds out that faith in a wizard is misplaced and that the answer to her problem lies within herself. For Dorothy, and for you, dreams really do come true — if you dare to dream.

[1]Glenn Van Ekeren, **The Speaker's Sourcebook**, "What Good Did It Do?", p. 57.

[2]Ibid., p. 54.

[3]Ibid., p. 66.

[4]Dwight Carlson, M.D., **Overcoming Hurts and Anger** (Harvest House Publishers, 1981), pp. 82, 85, 87.

[5]Ibid., 59.

Chapter 11

If Someone Else
Works For You

---

*"Sometimes the Lord calms the storm; sometimes He
lets the storm rage and calms His child."*

Anonymous

An advertising campaign by the First Nationwide Network once featured the slogan, "We will treat you with respect, concern and understanding, but don't worry. You'll get used to it." The somewhat cynical nature of this quote alludes to the apathetic, disrespectful treatment customers often receive from businesses. Employees frequently get the same treatment.

In a sense, employees are customers of their supervisors. When they perceive that the boss is treating them apathetically or disrespectfully, they become frustrated and disgruntled. Over time, they can easily become non-performing employees. It doesn't even matter whether their perception is an accurate representation of the facts. All that matters is how they feel.

While employees are busy making daily choices, supervisors are, too. Often, supervisors choose to do nothing. They allow employees to get by on their own, either sinking or swimming. Many simply fail to act out of insecurity. Other supervisors get in the way all the time, over-supervising and demanding respect they haven't earned.

The best supervisors do something else: They observe their subordinates and step in to help when there is a problem, but they do it in a supportive way. They help employees overcome obstacles and get back on track. They give the employee credit for the success. True builders such as these are rare, so appreciate them when you encounter one.

Good supervisors are just as sensitive to the needs of their subordinates as good salespeople are to the needs of their customers. They start relationships with a good foundation, then ongoing sensitivity helps them manage relationships in a productive, positive way. With healthy relationships, we can help our employees maneuver through the four phases of attitude in ways that are beneficial to them, our companies and ourselves.

To get relationships off to a good start, we can use the following guidelines derived from the four phases of attitude concept:

1. *Surround yourself with committed people.* It is always better to start by picking committed people in the first place. In other words, we want to avoid picking uncommitted people for our work unit. This is the fundamental secret of having motivated employees. It is much easier for a manager to inspire people who are motivated to begin with.

How do we find committed people? We look for people who are in an EXCITEMENT phase when we first meet them, and we inquire about their ability to stay in an EXCITEMENT phase without external help. Does their history show that they generally follow the positive path of the cycle, or will they need a lot of coaching? If you think they will need lots of coaching, you might want to pass them over. As they say in Las Vegas, "Never bet on a loser because you think his luck is bound to change."

2. *Establish commitment.* Having selected a person who believes in commitment, we next want to establish a solid commitment to our firm (or project or marriage) up front and preferably in writing. Take the short amount of time it requires to write out the original dream. That way, we can all refer back to the dream when FRUSTRATION comes along, and we'll be able to help the employee re-dream the dream during the RECOMMITMENT phase of the cycle.[1]

These points will help us understand why this is such an important step:

• Motivation stems from what we are committed to. If there is no commitment, there can be no motivation.

• The EXCITEMENT phase begins with a vision and a commitment to that vision. Without a commitment, there can be no excitement to start with or any to recommit to. To help others through FRUSTRATION, remind them of their commitment, their vision and their original EXCITEMENT.

3. *Be a motivational coach.* After they start, keep employees in an EXCITEMENT phase as much as possible by periodically reminding them of their vision, offering them frequent inspiration and encouragement and helping them to quickly exit the FRUSTRATION phase through RECOMMITMENT. This requires staying close to them (being alert, sensitive and empathetic). The most successful leaders in history have all been very effective at this. They clearly communicate a vision to those who would follow them, then work hard to establish and maintain the commitment of their followers to that vision. This advice applies equally well when

working with children, spouses and friends.

4. *Be worthy of emulation.* Since modelling is the most powerful learning tool on earth, it will be very helpful if you consciously model the four phases yourself, staying alert to your own FRUSTRATION and trying to maintain your vision, commitment and EXCITEMENT in visible ways.

5. *Ensure that people are committed.* At times, an employee may become a source of real frustration to you personally or to others in your organization. When this happens, we should help employees look for a more suitable project or career instead of just letting them go. This maintains their self-esteem, whereas getting fired does not. It also enhances our ability to work with them in the future, should that become necessary or desirable.

Using these concepts as our foundation, we then practice successful, ongoing supervision using the following three principles. These principles are essential for quality relationships. They apply equally well to relationships between bosses and employees, companies and customers, parents and children and between spouses.

Key number 1: We have to **be sensitive and alert to the signs of FRUSTRATION.** As we have seen, FRUSTRATION cycles in and out, as regular as rain. But when there's a downpour, we could have a flash flood on our hands, and the employee may seek to escape by LOOKING for another job or relationship. Stay on the alert if you want to prevent the loss of good employees.

Key number 2: We have to **listen and empathize** when we find FRUSTRATION. We cannot simply assume the other person needs an attitude adjustment or that he or she will get back on track without us. As supervisors, we can and should be proactive, looking for the signs of frustration and taking action when we find it. We need to encourage others to review their problems with us, but without getting defensive ourselves. We don't need to add to their fear.

An anonymous saying offers some additional advice: "Dig the well before you are thirsty." In other words, make sure your employees (and customers and children and spouses) feel comfortable about coming to you at all times, not just in times of crisis. We are all humans, with human emotions. We want someone to care about us as individuals. If this need is not satisfied, our frustration grows faster and deeper. When this need is satisfied, our EXCITEMENT has deeper roots and longer seasons.

Key number 3: **Take action to help the employee cope.** This may only require a fireside chat, where you provide the opportunity for the employee to vent his or her frustration. At other times, you will need to help the employee walk through the RECOMMITMENT forest back into EXCITE-MENT. There will also be times when you need to help them remove the obstacle(s) in the way. When there is some substance to the employee's or customer's fear, the best course of action is to help them, either by using our supervisory power to remove the obstacle or by helping them understand why it has to continue to exist, and how to cope. Employees can tolerate a great deal of frustration provided they know a supervisor shares their viewpoint and will take action when circumstances permit. It might be helpful to review the chapter on being an employee so that you will understand how to help employees help themselves.

LOOKING FOR CLUES

When we drive down the highway, we frequently have to stop and refuel the tank. People are no different. We need to keep our tank of commitment topped off in order to proceed along life's highway.

As a supervisor, you now know that employees will periodically require a reinjection of commitment and periodic looks at the corporate vision map. Just as a good driver would do, good supervisors plan for occasional pit stops, and you need to be watching the fuel gauges of your employees (and customers).

A clue that an employee needs your attention is when you notice a long-term, productive employee starting to have a productivity problem. Perhaps they are not getting the results they are accustomed to but haven't said anything to you about it. Perhaps they are beginning to blame external people, events and organizations for their failure. This would seem to suggest that they are going through FRUSTRATION and are in need of counseling from you. Customers exhibit the same behavior, but instead of lowering their productivity, they reduce the volume or size of orders. Instead of complaining directly to you, they complain to your delivery person, your receptionist or your sales rep. And when you don't listen, your competitor gets a chance to earn their business.

Another clue to look for is negative, complaining-type behavior. This can be observed as people interact with each other. It can surface in memos. And in its most subtle form, it is practiced by dropping hints. The hints might be dropped directly in front of you, or they might be dropped to someone the complainer thinks you listen to.

Missed deadlines or inadequate progress on projects are other signals of a slipping commitment level. An alert supervisor will pick up on these tidbits when appropriate and shrewdly use them to strengthen a relationship with the complaining employee or customer.

TAKING ACTION WHEN YOU DISCOVER FRUSTRATION

What can the boss do when it is apparent that an employee is in FRUSTRATION, or perhaps the subphase of anger? Sometimes, the boss is the first to notice and can head off a mole hill growing into a mountain. You can start out with an observation and follow it up with a conversation-starting question. For example, "Bill, I couldn't help but notice how you just handled that situation. Would you like to talk about what's bothering you?"

Hopefully, the employee (or customer) will open up and let you help, but you can expect them to be apprehensive and defensive the first several times you try this technique. Polite, caring persistence will ultimately pay off, and you should be able to get the root cause out on the table. Then, the issue you must resolve is whether the obstacles they are facing are real or imagined. If they are real, you must help them remove the obstacles. You might have to take some action yourself, such as authorizing additional spending, supplying helpful resources or providing outside training. If the obstacles are imaginary, you need to coach the employee past the obstacle and back through RECOMMITMENT. You might also be able to help:

... by analyzing the work load and making adjustments if possible;

... by reassigning a person to a mutually beneficial new role;

... by removing an employee that everyone knows is not pulling his or her weight;

... by removing an employee that is a trouble maker;

... by coaching the employee past the fear and back into the game; or

119

... by making strategic game plan changes or other changes only a boss can make.

If this sounds too simple, that's good because it doesn't need to be complicated. It's really just common-sense supervision, but as we all know, there's nothing common about common sense.

MISTAKES TO AVOID

Failure to do anything about legitimate complaints. Someone once told me an interesting story about a monastery in Spain. Young men who want to be part of the religious order there must maintain silence, so it takes a very disciplined spirit to endure this monastery. Every two years, the participants are allowed to speak, but they may only say two words.

One young man completed his first two years of training and was invited by his superior to make his first two-word presentation. "Food greasy," he said. Two years later, he received another invitation to speak. This time he said, "Bed uncomfortable." At the end of the sixth year, he proclaimed to his superior, "I quit." The superior looked at the young monk and said, "You know, this doesn't surprise me at all. Since you've been here, you've done nothing but complain, complain, complain."[2]

Is this story true? I don't really know. But if you were asked to describe your life in two words, what would you say? Would you focus on the rocks and walls and unfairness in your life, or would you point to the joy and happiness and discovery and wonder?

To me, this story also illustrates what I consider to be the typical tendency of an employee to complain and the typical tendency of an employer to respond as if the complaints had no merit. (Did the food change? Did the bed get changed?

Would the young monk have quit if they had? He did stick it out for six years, so he must have been very committed to his vision.)

As the supervisor in a situation like this, what would you do? Would you ignore the complaints and assume it was just the employee's negative attitude at work? Or would you take action? At the very least, you should explain to the employee that you care about the complaint and that when time and resources permit, you will take action to deal with the problem.

In the example above, the young monk chose to quit. His FRUSTRATION gave way to LOOKING because external causes were at fault. It resulted in turnover for the monastery. Some turnover in organizations is beneficial because it brings in new blood and fresh commitment, but turnover has many detrimental aspects, as well. It takes a lot of resources to attract, recruit, hire and train new employees. With turnover, experience is lost, and inexperience takes its place. Temporary EXCITEMENT replaces FRUSTRATION, and for a while things, will seem normal again, but unless the real cause of the frustration is eventually removed, turnover will probably come back again and again — spiraling down on top of you — in the same way that the negative path of the four phases can spiral your life out of control.

Failure to recognize frustration for what it really is. Many times, even supervisors who mean well can misread a situation. I once knew an employee who was a good, solid producer and manager, proven by the fact that he was up several times for promotion during his career. Company supervisors imposed restrictions: They wouldn't let him hire people when he thought it was necessary, thereby taking control away from him. For a while, he repressed most of the anger, directing it inwardly. (He tried to see it their way and still get the job done). After two years, his unresolved frustration had festered too long, so the anger changed from inwardly directed to outwardly directed. He started blaming his superiors, which, of course, they didn't like. Mistaking this high level of unresolved frustration for a bad attitude, they sought to relocate him to another place in the organization, where he would be with someone else, someone who wanted a doer and was willing to put up with the problem. Instead, he removed himself from the organization. The frustrations were real. Helping the employee remove them would have saved a good employee.

Frustrating policies. Another lesson of the previous story is that an employee's frustration can often be induced by an organization's rules and/or policies. If the realities of a frustration-producing condition are not recognized, many good employees (or customers) can be lost.

Let me give you another example of the frustrating power of a bad policy. I once moved the copier out of my secretary's office into the hallway so that she would not be repeatedly interrupted by people seeking to make copies. The new visibility of the copier soon led me to conclude that my people were making too many copies. To counteract this seemingly expensive phenomenon, I instituted a rule that only my administrative assistant could make copies, and anyone else would have to ask him to do it for them. I didn't realize how frustrating this policy could be until an associate pointed out one day that some of my people were taking work over to a local copy service because they could not get my administrative assistant to make the copies when they needed them. Their frustration over my policy was causing them to behave in ways that were not only unproductive for my organization but also economically disadvantageous.

The right supervisory action is to get rid of frustrating policies. Identifying them is easy. Just ask your employees what frustrates them. They will also be more than happy to suggest a variety of possible changes to make things better. Then, you can choose among the solutions they present. As Winston Churchill said during World War II, "Give us the tools, and we will finish the job." Remember, also, that asking others for solutions will help them travel the road through RE-COMMITMENT and on to EXCITEMENT.

Frustrating goals. Another danger zone for supervisors is the area of goal-setting. As you will recall, the energy behind our EXCITEMENT phase comes from our commitment to a worthwhile goal and our vision that this goal can be accomplished. If and when it becomes apparent that the goal is unrealistic, then FRUSTRATION will be deep and difficult to reverse.

In many organizations, unrealistic goals are a frequent root cause of frustrated employees. Roger Staubach tells a story about the Dallas Cowboys that relates to appropriate goal setting.

He describes the team at a point when it was a far cry from being a Super Bowl contender. Had the coach started the season with a goal of playing in the Super Bowl, it would have been only a matter of weeks before the players were all frustrated because they weren't quite ready to compete on that level. Instead, the coach set realistic goals for the team, goals that could be achieved with a fair amount of work. When these goals were achieved, the team was self-motivated. They were able to stay in an EXCITEMENT phase as they moved on to ever higher goals.

Several years later, the Cowboys won the Super Bowl. But they only reached for the Super Bowl when they were ready, willing and able to do so. Goals can frustrate, or they can inspire. As a supervisor, you have the power to choose which way it will be.

Most people would agree that the late Paul "Bear" Bryant of the University of Alabama was another superb coach. He knew how to lead, and he knew how to motivate his players. Each year, he would incorporate the goals of each player into his master plan for the team. He believed that when players saw how achieving the team goals would also achieve their own individual goals, they would be more apt to do what was necessary for the team to win. His tradition of winning football games is proof positive that his philosophy of supervision was a winner.

Frustrating incentive systems. If you are a hungry horse and someone hangs a carrot in front of you, you will be motivated to walk toward the carrot, even if it means pulling a heavy load while you walk. As a human being, you will respond to a variety of incentive systems, too, and you will pull a wagon in the direction of a carrot for a while. But humans are smarter than horses, and when we figure out that a game is rigged — that the carrot can never be reached — we will quickly become frustrated. Unlike horses, who will go quietly to the barn, only to fall for the same trick tomorrow, we humans will develop resentment towards game players, and we will respond in a variety of negative ways to the goals of Machiavellian masters.

Many excellent companies understand the delicate balance between the motivating power and the frustrating power of incentives. They deliberately design their incentive systems so that a large majority of their people will achieve success. More people reaching goals means more people in EXCITEMENT instead of FRUSTRATION. Excited employees reach for higher levels of performance. Frustrated employees reach for excuses.

Failure to hold people accountable. For years, I have asked a variety of leaders and managers what they believe are the two most important things they can do to make their careers easier and more productive. The answers I get range from ridiculous to wise, but I believe the best answer is as follows: "Delegate, and then hold people accountable."

Many supervisors delegate — and so do parents — but they frequently fail to hold the delegatee or child accountable for results. They accept poor performance, often letting the employee or child off the hook altogether. This leads to increased frustration on the supervisor's part, who usually has to work harder to get desired results, and it also leads to increased frustration for all of the employees or siblings who see someone else "getting away with murder."

Holding people accountable for higher results can also help build higher frustration-tolerance levels, provided that it is done in a supportive way. Good supervisors hold people accountable, building those people and getting results at the same time. As Goethe said, "When we treat a man as he is, we make him worse than he is. When we treat him as if he already were what he potentially could be, we make him what he should be."

GROUPS AND THE CYCLE

Organizations, businesses, teams and groups are collections of individual people. In the same way that Bear Bryant's teams took on the individual goals of the players to synthesize a team goal, the attitude of these collections of people takes on the characteristic attitudes of the individuals involved. In this sense, a group, a department, a company, a city, a state or even a whole country of people will have an attitude. This means that each of these entities will go through the four phases, just like you and I do.

Nowhere is this more evident than in the national political

arena. The attitude of the American people cycles back and forth between FRUSTRATION and EXCITEMENT, just as it does for individuals. When national elections take place, the fate of an incumbent often rises and falls with the prevailing attitudinal phase. If the majority is in an EXCITEMENT phase, the incumbent is reelected. If, on the other hand, the majority is deeply frustrated, the electorate is LOOKING for a way out of that frustration. This usually spells disaster for the incumbent.

The lesson for us as supervisors is simple. First, we need to recognize that groups and organizations follow the four phases, too. Second, we need to be alert as to what phase our groups are in so we can provide appropriate leadership. When a group is in EXCITEMENT, it's fairly easy to keep it there. But when a group is in FRUSTRATION, it often takes real leadership to bring the attitude of the group through RECOMMITMENT and back to EXCITEMENT. But if we have been practicing the principles reviewed in this chapter, then we are well on our way to being good leaders.

CONCLUSION

In summary, if you want to be a successful supervisor, pick committed, enthusiastic people. Set realistic goals, and be a good role model yourself. Keep the dreams of your employees focused for them. Be alert to any signs of frustration, and remove real frustrations whenever possible. Lead them regularly on a walk through the recommitment forest. Then watch them leap over, walk around, duck under or just break straight through to success!

[1]Refer to the sample commitment form in the appendix, with What?, Why?, My Dream, My Reward.
[2]Glenn Van Ekeren, **The Speaker's Sourcebook**, "Complain! Complain! Complain!" pp. 62-63.

Chapter 12

Common Ground: Other Areas of Life

"Ability is what you're capable of doing. Motivation determines what you do. Attitude determines how well you do it."

Lou Holtz

"Every beginning is hard."

From the German

You're probably saying, "Okay, Jim. So far, so good. This is pretty good stuff for my career and my company. But there's a lot more to life than that. How does this cycle of attitude fit with the rest of my life?"

My answer is that it fits in with every aspect of life. In this chapter, I'll give you a variety of examples to help you apply the four-phases concept in your own life. We can use this cycle to help us handle family problems, selling situations, loss of morale, financial setbacks and more. It can also help us handle all of the emotions related to the death of a loved one, a divorce, family illness or other setbacks from health-related causes.

As our first example, let's consider the experience of Dr. Victor Frankl, author of the famous book, **Man's Search for Meaning**. This first example deals with a long-term situation, fraught with daily frustration and incredibly difficult problems.

Imagine this: Your family is taken away. You are stripped of all your personal belongings: Your home, your possessions, your watch, even your wedding ring is gone. Your head is shaved and all of your clothes removed, after which you are marched into a Gestapo courtroom. Falsely accused and interrogated by the German high command, you are found guilty of their charges and taken to a concentration camp. You expect years of indignity and humiliation to follow. With no hope, and no light at the end of the tunnel, you decide to give up. Right? Many of us would, but it need not be.[1]

Dr. Frankl experienced some of the worst events humans can imagine; however, he realized he had the power to choose one thing — his attitude. No matter what the future had in store for him, he knew he could choose his state of mind. As you review each of the following questions, questions that Dr. Frankl might have asked, ask yourself how you would respond in a similar situation.

Do I throw in the towel and die, or do I persevere so I can fulfill my dreams?

Do I hate the Gestapo command or forgive them?

Do I succumb to a world of deprivation and self-pity or endure the hardships?

Dr. Frankl chose to exist in a different world; a world he created in his mind. His attitude sustained him. He survived and was finally liberated. He went on to pursue his unfinished goal.

How does the four-phases concept apply to this? Let's review what we know.

Given his situation, could Dr. Frankl possibly have been in an EXCITEMENT phase? He might have been in one before being taken by the Gestapo, but odds are pretty good that, by the time he arrived at the concentration camp, he was a little bit FRUSTRATED. There was undoubtedly some SHOCK at being in the situation, a lot of DENIAL and a great deal of FEAR and apprehension.

Do you think he experienced any ANGER? Did he move on to JUSTIFICATION and ACCEPTANCE? Many of the prisoners did. They took the negative path — maybe they fought it off for a while, but eventually many went LOOK-ING for a way out — dying in the process. Not Frankl. He chose the positive path of RECOMMITMENT.

First, he redreamed the dream of a happy life, one outside of the camp. Then, he set some goals for himself: the long-term goal of writing a book about his experiences and short-term goals of making it through each day, making note of significant experiences and carefully observing his fellow prisoners. Finally, he sought the help of his fellow prisoners as red-flag partners and mentors. As red-flag partners, they helped him make daily progress toward his dream by supplying information and helping to restore his attitude on occasion. As mentors, they helped guide him back to happy times and gave him the insight necessary to write his book.

How many times do you think he went through the cycle during his years in captivity? Once? Twice? Three times? My guess is that he went through the cycle hundreds, if not thousands of times — and probably several times a day. Like the rest of us, he undoubtedly followed the negative side of the cycle from time to time, finding some sort of perverse EXCITEMENT in the thought of giving up and letting go.

But each time, he must have realized that as emotionally easy as that might have been, it wouldn't be nearly as satisfying as beating the odds — living in spite of Hitler's atrocities, living to see his family again, and living to write about his experiences.

FAMILY LIFE

In reviewing my personal experiences with this four-phases concept, I've noticed that my own attitude often goes from the positive side to the negative side so quickly that before I know it, I am in trouble and not sure how I got there. This next example, told to me by a close friend of mine, illustrates how quickly we can switch from EXCITEMENT to FRUS-TRATION and back again.

"Just this morning, I was holding my 5-month-old son. My wife had been up all night feeding and holding him, and she was trying to catch an hour or two of much-needed sleep. I started off EXCITED about the opportunity to do my part by holding him and spending time with him, but when he started crying, it wasn't long before my EXCITEMENT turned into FRUSTRATION. No matter what I did, I couldn't keep him from crying for long. I was SHOCKED by the difficulty of this simple assignment. And I certainly went through a quick phase of DENIAL because I knew I wasn't causing the problem. The baby was!

"DENIAL turned to FEAR as my mind began to wander. I began to think about having to carry him around all day to keep him from crying. I also began to fear the thought that I might not be able to get any productive work done because I was falling behind in my schedule.

"Then, my fears turned into strong emotions of ANGER, which I had a great deal of difficulty controlling. My first impulse was to be angry at the baby, and I found myself saying things like, 'Stop it. Don't do this to me. You've got to stop crying.' At one point, the ANGER was so strong I even thought about throwing the baby down to get it to stop. I wanted to scream, but I knew that wouldn't do any good, either.

"Then I turned my ANGER toward my wife. How could she do this to me? Why wasn't she coming to my aid and asking to take the baby? I wanted out of this experience. I wanted the FRUSTRATION to go away and began thinking about ways to accomplish this new goal. I JUSTIFIED my position by saying to myself, 'This is my wife's responsibility, not mine. I'm supposed to be working on other things.'

"Then I caught myself. Aware of the four phases of attitude, I suddenly realized that I was angry. Deciding that I would use what I knew to get my attitude back to where it belonged, I started to think about realistic solutions to my problem, quickly settling on the age-old technique of singing the child to sleep. Ten minutes later, I was back in control of my life. I am convinced that redirecting the energy of my anger toward removing the source of my frustration was more productive for me than remaining angry at the world would have been."

THE FRUSTRATION OF SELLING

Here is another real-life example of how the four phases can help. This time it is a salesperson experiencing the all-too-common frustration of sales.

"Reading the newspaper one day, I noticed an ad for a free seminar on living trusts. Never one to pass up something for free, I decided to go. At the seminar, I met a lady who was trying to solve some financial problems in her life. As I got to know her, I realized she needed help overcoming her fear of investing. Subsequent conversations went well, and I felt we were moving toward progress for her and a sale for me. I was in an EXCITEMENT phase, and I was productive.

"We started out by reviewing her current situation. It rapidly became apparent that she was relying too heavily on safe certificates of deposit. I made several suggestions which she seemed to take interest in. Later, we were talking about how she could work with her bank to improve her situation temporarily, giving us more time to work on a long-term solution. In trying to help her, I was inadvertently making the mistake of sending her in the direction of a competitor! She went to the bank, coming back with an offer from them that she said she couldn't refuse. They had essentially doubled her safe return, making it much harder for her to overcome her fear of taking any investment risk. Since she had tied up her money for two years, my sale sailed out the window.

"I immediately shifted into FRUSTRATION. I was SHOCKED that this could be happening to me and that she would turn to someone else after all the help I had given her. Naturally, I began to DENY any responsibility for the problem, blaming it instead on the low interest rates I currently had to offer, our lack of more competitive product solutions and my boss. I was driving down the street with my wife on the way to pick up dinner, just going on and on about the situation. I was expressing discouragement at every turn, which led me to ask, 'What if all the prospects out there treat me this way?' This was followed by the unpleasant answer, 'I'll never reach my sales quota.'

"FEAR began to enter my picture, telling me I might not achieve our income needs, that I might not be able to hold my job, that I wouldn't be successful. ANGER began to rise inside of me, and I began to express it by driving faster. I glared out at other motorists who seemed to be moving like molasses. My little boy in the back seat seemed to be a constant aggravation instead of the incredible joy he really is. My mind was racing and looking for a solution to the problems I faced. I even began to talk about quitting, expressing thoughts to my wife about how I might JUSTIFY this to myself, my friends and my relatives.

"And then it hit me. I was caught up in the cycle, and I was heading down the path to destruction. It was my own attitude that was the problem — not the prospect, not the competition, not my company, not my boss. As I began to turn the ANGER towards a positive solution, I reflected on my past accomplishments. I had made plenty of sales, and all I had to do was make another one. More reflection caused me to admit that I really hadn't been making enough sales calls to get the job done. I began to redream the dream of a successful career, complete with high commissions, lots of satisfied clients and the success that other sales representatives with our company enjoy.

"It was all up to me. I recommitted myself to my original goal and then set a short-term goal to find another way to reach this client. I went home and wrote a note to her, then set about analyzing the situation all over again. I asked my wife for help. She became my mentor, helping me to look for alternative solutions. What did I do wrong? What could I do to reintroduce the subject without being pushy? How could I turn failure into success?

"I must confess that I never did sell anything to this lady, but I did earn recognition as sales representative of the month for the next two months running and wound up the year in the top 10. I couldn't have done that without redirecting my attitude."

PROJECTS: WRITING THIS BOOK

As anyone who has tried it can attest, writing a book is a long-term project. Rome wasn't built in a day, and books aren't written that quickly, either. This book took nearly 15 years, and it serves as a perfect example of how both cycles of the four-phases concept apply to long-term projects.

When I first decided to create a book, I realized I didn't have the ability to write it by myself, so I was smart enough to delegate this responsibility. Unfortunately, I was not very proficient in choosing my delegatees. Time after time, I would get someone involved in the project, and time after time, they would hit the wall of FRUSTRATION and quit. In all fairness, I have to say that I might not have been a very supportive boss throughout the process, but regardless of the specifics, the negative half of the cycle came up repeatedly as each would-be writer went LOOKING for some other source of EXCITEMENT.

As evidenced by the fact that you are reading this, the project was finally completed. Even so, it took us well over seven years to reach the point where we felt the product was suitable for publication. The writer who assisted me confessed that he went through the cycle hundreds of times during the project. At times, we went through it together, with one or the other of us acting as the red-flag partner. What made the difference, and resulted in this finished product, was that neither one of us ever considered taking the negative path. This just goes to show that we all must be students of successful attitude-management strategies and that we all struggle with the process, even when we understand it well.

Each time we hit the wall of FRUSTRATION, we knew that the answer was recommitting to the project and getting back into EXCITEMENT by redreaming the dream of a published book and the many people that might find it helpful. Many times, we set short-term goals to get together or complete various sections of the book. Many times, we prevailed on various mentors to guide us in the subtle details of writing. Sometimes, the phase of RECOMMITMENT went by quickly. Other times, it literally took months.

For what it's worth, neither one of us makes our living as a writer, so it's not really surprising that it took that long. It does serve to point out how the time spent in each phase can vary dramatically and that it has little effect on the outcome. What does matter is the commitment and the up-front decision to recommit as many times as necessary until the project is successfully behind you.

EVERYDAY LIFE

Recently, I was driving down the interstate with my family on my way back to town. It was raining cats and dogs and elephants, and it was hard to see. I wanted to get home quickly, and we were making pretty good headway until I caught up with a couple of 18 wheelers. One was in the left lane, and the other was staggered in front on the right. If you've spent any time at all on the highway, then you know how much water the wheels of a truck throw out to the sides and to the back. My windshield wipers were already working double overtime from the rain, and now they had to contend with a waterfall, too. Throw in the fact that there was no way to get around those two lane-blocking behemoths, and you've got the makings of first-class frustration for a time-conscious person like me.

My trip through SHOCK, DENIAL and FEAR was extremely rapid. Quick as you please, I was in the anger subphase; with outwardly directed anger at my side. And who do you think the target was? That's right — the truck drivers. In my mind, they had no business hogging both lanes like that. And besides, they ought to be polite and pull over instead of blocking traffic and throwing up all that extra water. Why did it have to be raining, anyway?

Time out! What am I doing? You're right! I'm blaming everything and everybody else but me. Let's back up for a second, like I did that day on the interstate (mentally, not physically). What was my goal? You're right, again. It was to get home safely. My dream is a happy family, and that isn't compatible with a wreck on the interstate. Once I realized this, I eased up on the gas pedal and decided to accept the conditions I was facing. There simply wasn't anything I could do about them except to remove the FEAR of getting home a few minutes later than I'd hoped.

Seconds later, I was safely following 10 car lengths behind the trucks and happily experiencing a renewed EXCITEMENT phase. My FRUSTRATION was gone.

MARRIAGE AND RELATIONSHIPS

Ah, marriage. *C'est magnifique* — that marvelous moment when two people commit to honor and cherish each other for life. Such EXCITEMENT! What wonderful dreams! What a beautiful commitment!

But, as all of us know, living in the same house or apartment with someone else eventually leads to a little conflict here and there. Throw in the pressure of jobs, the pressures of money, the strain of young children, a pinch of in-law trouble and you have a witch's brew of FRUSTRATION beyond compare. Is it any wonder that we throw really big parties for couples who make it all the way to 50 years of marriage?

Much of what has been said in previous chapters applies to close personal relationships. There will be many frustrations to deal with — some real and some imaginary — and as with every other example, these must be dealt with, one at a time as they come up. The important thing to remember is that each person brings some degree of commitment to the relationship.

In the case of a friendship, the commitment may or may not be very deep. In the case of a marriage, it should be very strong. It's up to you to decide, but it's also the critical factor in determining how healthy your relationship will be because your original commitment to each other will be the well spring for RECOMMITMENT. Couples who take their marriage vows seriously will be more likely to stay together because they have a lot to work with. Couples who simply go through the motions or never really commit to the goal of a healthy relationship will have a much more difficult time.

OTHER AREAS OF LIFE

There are many other areas of life that we could discuss, but by now, you should have a pretty good idea of what's involved. Investors who don't see early results and get frustrated need to RECOMMIT to their original goals. People trying to lose weight have to make sure they are solidly committed and ready to deal with all of the FEAR. Athletes who don't make the team need to keep trying. People who have gotten out of the habit of going to church or who have lost their faith in God need to RECOMMIT to the spiritual needs they have. And so on.

Achieving success at anything we choose is not really that complicated. We tend to complicate it ourselves, perhaps because so many books have been written about how to be a success. The truth is written in between the lines of every amazing new concept or philosophy that hits the market today. The bottom line is this: If you maintain your attitude in a positive way, recommitting at every frustrating point, everything you want to accomplish will come to pass. Or as Napoleon Hill once said, "Whatever the mind can conceive and believe, it can achieve."

There is no doubt in my mind, and probably none in your mind, either, that if there were some magic by which you could maintain your attitude on a positive side, under any amount of stress, during any crisis, during any social squabble, marital argument, irritation on the job or difficulty in other situations, your life would become a lot simpler, a lot happier and you would just be more successful. Well, unfortunately, there is no magic, at least not yet. But with an understanding of the cycle, we've got a better chance of making it happen than without it.

In the next chapter, I will show you how some Super Achievers used their understanding to make those right choices.

[1] Glenn Van Ekeren, **The Speaker's Sourcebook**, "You Choose." p. 59.

Chapter 13

Attitude of Super Achievers

"You can measure a man by the opposition it takes to discourage him."

Robert C. Savage

"The difference between a successful person and others is not a lack of strength, not a lack of knowledge, but rather in a lack of will."

Anonymous

"He is strong who conquers others; he who conquers himself is mighty."

Lao Tsu

"Fear was absolutely necessary. Without it, I would have been scared to death."

Former heavyweight champion Floyd Patterson

A ROSE BY ANY OTHER NAME

As we have seen, everyone in life experiences frustration. Everyone experiences problems, interruptions, barriers, hindrances, obstacles and impediments. But why do some people rise above these things to become Super Achievers, while others simply fall by the wayside? What is the ultimate secret of success?

One theory is that Super Achievers have an overwhelming sense of mission, a strong purpose in life, something that keeps their mental focus out in the distance. This allows them to simply walk over, under, around or through any obstacle in their path to their dream. While this is undoubtedly quite valid, I would contend that these Super Achievers are able to get around the obstacles because they are unconsciously good at making the right split-second choices in life.

Repeatedly making the choice to direct the forces of frustration and anger toward positive solutions and to take personal responsibility for dealing with problems masquerades by many names, including perseverance, will power, indomitable spirit, persistence and determination.

Belief in the power of perseverance has led to such familiar axioms as:
- If at first you don't succeed, try, try again.
- Hang in there!
- Never, never, never quit!
- Fall seven times, stand up eight!
- The man who fights one more round is never beaten.
- A man can fail many times, but he is not a failure until he gives up.
- Our greatest glory is not in never falling, but in rising

every time we fall.

Evidence of these ideas can be seen in the lives of every successful person, but if you look carefully between the lines, you'll see that these are the effects, not the cause. The root cause that leads to success through perseverance is the decision to take personal responsibility for achieving the results.

In this chapter, we will have the opportunity to see how several Super Achievers use the four phases of attitude concept in their lives.

Let's take a look at these examples and see if we can spot the secret of success in each case.

W. R. "SKIP" BLACK

I wish you could have the pleasure of meeting Skip Black. What a refreshing experience it would be for you. He is one of the most inspiring individuals you could ever hope to run across.

Skip was born in 1953. As a young boy, he experienced several episodes of pneumonia, and when his grandfather urged the family doctor to give Skip a shot of penicillin, he was sent to the University of Alabama in Birmingham for a more complete diagnosis. At the age of 9, Skip was told that he had Duchenne's Muscular Dystrophy. This is the disease made famous by Jerry Lewis and his telethons. The prognosis is very poor and almost always leads to respiratory problems, so Skip was not expected to live very long. It was a traumatic moment for his parents and very difficult for his mother to accept, but his father declared, "We'll just make the best of it."

When Skip was in the ninth grade, his parents moved to a small town, and the public school there was housed in an older building with 10 or 12 steps leading to the front entrance. Although Skip was mobile and able to walk, it was very difficult for him to climb stairs of any kind. There was no alternative way for him to receive an education in those days, and since he wasn't expected to live much longer, his parents and doctors agreed it was best for him to simply drop out of school.

As Skip puts it, he is "not the kind of person to just sit around and do nothing," so he put his joy for reading to work and went to the library a lot. With the help of books and public television, he educated himself. He learned to cook and worked at various hobbies and crafts. Among his many talents, Skip is an accomplished wildlife artist. His paintings are simply magnificent.

At the age of 26, Skip fell and fractured his hip. He was home alone at the time and lay on the floor for more than 12 hours before his mother returned home to find him. The doctor said it was one of the worst fractures he had ever seen and that it was a miracle Skip hadn't bled to death. The operation involved putting a pin into his hip, and it threw his balance off so much that he finally had to start using a wheelchair. You can just imagine the disappointment and frustration this caused Skip. He had fought and struggled to stay mobile, and the wheelchair was very difficult for him to accept. But this is where Skip Black's attitude comes into play. He chose to put a positive spin on the situation. Now he didn't have to worry about falling or having somebody bump into him.

At 32, Skip's family transferred to Baton Rouge, Louisiana. Although Skip was doing very well with his wildlife painting, he wanted more out of life. He had lived more than twice as long as the doctors had expected, so he decided to explore his alternatives.

After taking the high school equivalency exam and earning his general equivalency diploma, Skip went to a neuro-logical specialist. He was rediagnosed as having Becker's Dystrophy, a milder form of dystrophy than Duchenne's. His condition was stable, his heart was healthy and he was told that he could look forward to a normal life span.

Skip decided to get a college degree. He took the ACT exam and applied to Louisiana State University. Determined to graduate in four years, Skip took more class hours than his advisors recommended and went to school during the summers. Four years later, he received his undergraduate degree in accounting. Then he enrolled in law school, graduating in 1994 and earning the right to practice law in 1995. Today, he drives a specially equipped van and works in his own law office.

Before Skip was able to achieve the goal of having that specially equipped van, he was dependent on friends and family for transportation. Can you imagine the frustration he must have experienced in the pursuit of his educational goals? "It meant I had to be flexible," he said of those days. "I could make it negative, and say, 'Well, I can't go,' and those type of things. But we were able to work together. With my family and friends, whatever I've needed to do, I've always been able to be there and be on time. It has taught me to have a lot of patience and to be accommodating and at the same time to make sure that my needs get met."

What makes Skip Black a Super Achiever is the way in which he has succeeded in the face of obstacles and daily frustrations that would make most of us cry. You would expect someone in his position to blame others for all his troubles. But that's not Skip.

"I take responsibility for what I do and what I don't do," he said. "I'm not saying that sometimes other people don't become roadblocks, but I think a lot of times when they're roadblocks, it's our interaction with them, the way we're dealing with them. Maybe I'm not approaching them the right way. I'm not naive enough to say that there aren't people out in the world that sometimes just want to be ornery, don't want to get along with anybody. I just feel like I'm accountable for what I do, and I'm responsible for the decisions I make. It's not going to really benefit me to blame somebody else."

Skip describes his attitude this way: "As a person with a disability, attitude is one of the most important things a person can possess because no matter what your circumstances or your station in life, if you have a positive attitude, I think you're happier, and I think you're more complete and you can find real satisfaction in that. If you focus always on the negative, that brings you down as a person, makes you feel bad.

"I've always felt that I could look at my disability and say the negative: 'Well, I'm in a wheelchair, how bad that is, I can't go here, I can't do that,' or I can say, 'Hey, I'm in a wheelchair, that's my way I get about.' It doesn't hinder me from doing anything. My attitude hinders me. If I hold back and say, 'Aw, I'm in a wheelchair, nobody wants to be around me,' well, nobody's going to be around me. If you're positive, and you just go on — I have friends now, they say, 'Skip, I forgot you were even in a wheelchair.'"

Skip's office is next to mine, and one day I saw him rolling his wheelchair from his van to his office in the rain. He just looked up and waved to me as if the sun was shining. Now that's the attitude of a Super Achiever.

CAROLYN AND LARRY WARD

Carolyn is a national sales director for the Mary Kay organization, a position she has held since 1976. Attaining the position of national sales director means that she has been responsible for maintaining very high levels of business performance and for bringing at least 10 others up to a high level of management within the company. When Carolyn became a national sales director, she was in the top 10, and that is where she has been ever since. She is a charter member of the Millionaire Club and a Mary Kay Inner Circle Member.

This level of achievement has enabled Larry and Carolyn to travel around the world. They have flown on the Concorde, and they have ridden on the Orient Express. They own a beautiful home by a golf course. But as you might expect, it wasn't always that way.

In many respects, Larry and Carolyn's experience serves as a classic example of the attitude cycles we have discussed in this book. Early on, Carolyn's career path was characterized by numerous trips through the LOOKING glass, but when she decided to go to work as a Mary Kay consultant, she began to visit the RECOMMITMENT phase, instead.

Carolyn was a college student, but she quit. She went to work as a legal assistant, with illusions of grandeur, but quickly found the work to be hum drum. Accused of not doing her job properly, she quit. She got excited about her education again and tried going back to college, where she settled down long enough to try three different majors. Once again, after two years of frustration over the concept of studying, she got bored and made the split-second choice to quit.

Her next job was a secretarial one with two attorneys. She lasted six months. Accused again of not doing the job properly, she was fired. She moved on to a life insurance company, as the secretary to a claims adjuster. She was so understimulated by this job that she even fell asleep once during dictation. It was during this time she met Larry, a handsome young man stationed at Keesler Air Force Base.

Not long after that, she quit her job with the life insurance company to try yet another one someplace else.

Before she had time to settle in at her new location, Larry and Carolyn decided to marry. Shortly after the wedding, they were transferred to Glasgow, Montana, by the Air Force. The excitement of the transfer quickly gave way to frustration as the young married couple had to sleep without a mattress, suffer through the flu together, then pack for a three-month trip to California for the prerequisite training Larry needed.

Back in Glasgow, the young southern gal quickly ran into frustration again. Sixteen miles from the Canadian border, she hated the thought of being so far from her home, her parents and her friends. What kept her there was her love for Larry and her commitment to the marriage. Because she had this dream, the young couple made a conscious attempt to get to know others, to get involved and create an environment where they could be content. They hosted barbecues and played cards because, as Larry said, "You have to create memories."

From my point of view, it was here that Larry and Carolyn made the first split-second decision that changed their lives. They chose not to let their fear and anger overcome them. They had the dream of a happy marriage, and they reviewed it often. They set the short-term goal of getting involved, and intuitively, Larry became their mentor. Perhaps it was his Air Force training, but it was here that Larry first took on the role of being Carolyn's biggest supporter or, as she said, "the wind beneath my wings."

After three years in Glasgow, Larry and Carolyn were transferred to Abilene, Texas. Since Larry made a good living as an officer in the Air Force, Carolyn had chosen to work as a housewife. She also did volunteer work with the Red Cross and sang with a choir group. Two years after moving to Abilene, the Wards' next-door neighbor invited Carolyn to a demonstration of Mary Kay cosmetics at her home. Carolyn didn't want to go, but she did. She fell in love with the product, and bought it. At the same time, a tiny seed was planted when a girl at the meeting put her hand on Carolyn's shoulder and told her, "You would be great doing this." Carolyn, wearing Bermuda shorts, tennis shoes with holes in them and with her hair up in rollers, thought, "You've got to be stupid *and* blind."

She went home asking herself, "How can I tell Larry I just spent $15.95 on cosmetics?"

In a good-natured way, I'm sure, but frustrated nonetheless, Larry responded by saying there's "a sucker born every minute." In another split-second decision, anger toward his comment kicked in Carolyn's "I'll show you" determination, and she began to use the product faithfully. Several weeks later, Larry said, "I think the stuff is working. Your skin really looks soft and smooth. Why don't you take a job selling it?"

Carolyn didn't want to work. In particular, she didn't want a job in sales. Her father was in sales, and she didn't want anything to do with it. But later that night, she sat straight up in bed in a dark room, thinking, "I really can do this." She got very excited, thinking to herself, "I can do everything that girl did." She hit Larry, telling him she could do it. He told her to go back to sleep.

The next morning, she tried to find the girl from the demonstration, but she was gone. Undaunted by this frustration because of her excitement, Carolyn called the director, instead, and told her she wanted to buy the lotion she had seen at the demonstration. Wanting to check out the potential earnings, Carolyn insisted on going to the director's home to pick up the product. She asked too many questions about the business, and the director knew she was hooked. This time, it was the director who said to Carolyn, "You would be great doing this."

After a sales meeting and a meeting with the director, the director's husband and Larry, Carolyn was so excited she couldn't sleep. At Larry's urging, she bought $200 worth of inventory and started on yet another opportunity: a ground-floor opportunity with unlimited potential.

She ran into frustration at her first showing, because she only sold $1 worth of product. But her discouragement was offset by Larry's praise when he said, "That's great. I knew you could do it. You made it through the demonstration. That's the most important thing." Carolyn was recommitted to her goal and began to find success selling the product.

Not long after that, Larry and Carolyn moved to New Orleans, where frustration and fear struck again. Mary Kay Cosmetics was just three years old at the time, and Carolyn was the only representative in New Orleans. She didn't know anyone. Larry was taking a substantial cut in pay. How would she get her business going? She had to face a lot of rejection, do a lot of footwork and talk to a lot of people just to get one person to look at the product. But she knew that once she got people to put the product on their faces, it sold itself. She knew that if she talked to enough people, her problems would take care of themselves. She made up her mind to talk to enough people so that she and Larry could eat.

Carolyn was unconsciously recommitting to her dream and setting short-term goals. Deep in her subconscious, she knew that she had a real opportunity, and this was the underlying theme that helped her through those frustrating times.

The dream for Carolyn was the prospect of unlimited income. As she says, most jobs pay what the job is worth, but an opportunity with Mary Kay Cosmetics pays what you are worth. The Mary Kay organization also puts things in the order of priority that women truly value: God first, family second, and career third. After meeting Mary Kay Ash herself, Carolyn said she knew the woman really believed that her company would make a real difference in women's lives. And it has. Today, Mary Kay Cosmetics is represented in 24 countries around the world by over four hundred thousand representatives.

After some 10 months in the business, Carolyn was encouraged by her director to go to Dallas for the annual Mary Kay convention. There, she saw directors receiving $2,000 checks and walking across the stage in beautiful clothes. She thought, "What do they do that I can't do?" She wanted to be up there on that stage, the lights shining on her, jewels glittering, walking to that music.

After that dream was shown to her, she not only recommitted to her goals, she actually committed to a new, much more difficult goal. She decided to become a director before the end of the year and signed a letter of intent. This goal meant that Carolyn had to recruit nine more people in less than three months. But she was determined not to fail, and she did it.

To reach the next level, she had to recruit even more people. Do you think she faced any frustration in her task? Of course she did. People looked at her like she was crazy. She had to talk to lots of people, but she was in an EXCITEMENT phase. "Enthusiasm bypasses the conscious mind," she said. She was pumped, and nothing got in her way. She would talk to someone for an hour and a half, only to find out they didn't want to participate. She would say, "Oh, well, I sure am sorry." She felt the frustration, but she said to herself, "If I allow myself to go through that, I'm not going to get anywhere. So it's on to the next one."

As we've noted before, in the excitement phase, you can jump over, go around or just break through to success.

The big wall of frustration came in her first year as a director. In her words, it was "like a bulldozer." It was the wall of frustration that comes from dealing with people: when you find out that people don't want what you think they want; when they aren't going to live up to what you expect them to live up to.

She felt tremendous frustration and disappointment. She was stunned. She thought everyone was going to be like her, and she got angry. She would think, "You're so stupid if you can't see this opportunity."

For three years, she was in denial, saying, "It's not me, it's them. They just can't see the benefits." She went to her mother's house after a sales meeting one night, threw her briefcase on the couch and said, "I quit."

As soon as the words were out of her mouth, she knew she wouldn't really quit, but it felt good to say it. The disappointment in people was really hard to handle. Managing people was a whole new arena for her. It was not like selling the product. People needed motivation. She shed a lot of tears during those three years. Recommitment and short-term goals worked for a while, but it finally became time for an outside opinion.

After three years as a director, Carolyn asked for an appointment with her boss, Mary Kay Ash. Sitting on a footstool in Mary Kay's office, she cried for an hour. She carried on and on, telling Mary Kay about what everyone had done to her and how she had been hurt and how people didn't respect that she'd tried so hard. And on and on.

Like a good supervisor, Mary Kay Ash didn't say much in that hour. She mainly listened, nodding here and there, making a few comments at appropriate moments. She let Carolyn get it all out. She let her purge all her fear and her anger.

At the end of the hour, she said, "You know, Carolyn, when you grow up and realize that this is not a game of hearts and flowers, but a business, you'll make a fine director." In other words, she told her to stop blaming others for her problems and to take responsibility into her own hands.

It turned her around. Carolyn went home thinking, "Okay, now I have to grow up. It's my responsibility. It's up to me." RECOMMITTED and back in EXCITEMENT, she focused on getting one of her directors into qualification for the next level. She started seeing things in a different light, as if someone had pulled up a shade, and said, "Okay, now you can be a leader." That year, Carolyn was in the top 10 of directors companywide. Her career took off. She went all the way from receiving a letter saying she was about to be terminated for lack of production to being in the top 10.

At this point, you might be saying to yourself, "Wow. She really made a turnaround in her life. She went from being a person who was always quitting and looking for something else to a person who just recommits her way out of everything."

But you might also be asking, "I wonder if she ever came close to quitting?"

Well, she did come close — real close. She was having a particularly trying time with one of her consultants. It got so bad that Carolyn said, "If this is what I have to put up with, I don't know if I want it." Once again, recommitment and short-term goals weren't enough to snuff out the flame of frustration. But this time, Carolyn went to her father for her outside opinion. After she explained the situation and said, "I don't know what to do with her," her father gave her some very sage advice. He said, "Carolyn, it always takes two to argue. Become a ghost. If you don't respond, she can't fight."

Carolyn was still occasionally blaming others at that point in her career. She hadn't yet gained the strength to take on the responsibility of her own results.

She took her father's advice, and it was the second big turning point in her career. She was able to recommit and move back into EXCITEMENT.

Today, she puts all of this wisdom to work when she advises others. She also believes that praise and rewards are very important in helping people stay in the EXCITEMENT phase. She remembers the year she first made the top 10, receiving the gift of a Cadillac automobile from Mary Kay. Her father had always wanted a Cadillac, and as a kid, she grew up thinking that Cadillacs were the ultimate, so it was a dream come true to receive one.

She and Larry also read uplifting, inspiring books to help with their attitude. These books help overcome a lot of frustration because they help you say, "I'm not going to let this get me down."

When I asked Carolyn what advice she would give to others about controlling attitude and becoming successful, she told me the following: "Be very aware of these phases, and use that knowledge to your advantage. When you are strongly committed to something, the stages will be there, but they won't prevent you from achieving your goal if you understand how to work through them.

"With persistence and stick-to-it-iveness, you can see something through. You'll see results. You just have to hang in there. When you do, you'll see that it was a hard beginning, but over time comes a real good sense of balance, a leveling out point where wisdom begins to take hold. Many people strive for this, but they quit before they reach this position.

"When you stick it out — through persistence, commitment, discipline, and hard work — you'll be able to look out from the mountain top and see it, and it's a real good place to be."

GRIFF PICKARD

H. Griffin Pickard Jr. has been an achiever all of his life. In the Boy Scouts, he made Eagle Scout and earned the God and Country award. Later, he played on a winning football team. He cut grass and delivered papers, taking the profits down to the local bank, where he and his parents made a game out of buying U.S. savings bonds. In college, he earned a degree in pharmacology, and in the military, he became a pilot and an officer while serving his country in the Vietnam war.

After the war and a brief period as a pharmacist, Griff built a real estate business in Albuquerque, New Mexico. He started with an eight-unit apartment complex and traded his way into the commercial real estate market. One thing led to another, and by the late 1970s, Griff's business holdings included seven different businesses and a variety of other assets. In 1979, business was so good that his firm was able to close on 35 homes in one month.

But at the turn of the decade, the prime interest rate shot up to in excess of 20 percent, and with all of his businesses based on real estate and leveraged investments, Griff found himself paying more than $4,400 per day in interest — not just on weekdays, but on weekends and holidays, too. Instead of closing 35 homes in one month, he was having trouble closing one. In danger of losing everything, he and his wife sat down and made some tough decisions. Over the next year, they managed to sell enough assets and close enough creative deals to avoid closing their business.

After taking time to regroup and reassess their priorities,

Griff and his family continued to develop real estate in Albuquerque, and today, they enjoy continuing success from all of their hard work.

Naturally, Griff's attitude plays a big part in his success. When his business ran into difficulty in 1980, it would have been easy for him to blame it on outside forces like the change in government policies. Instead, he chose to look in the mirror and say, "I shouldn't have gotten into some of the things that I did, and now that I have, what can I do to work my way out of this?" He also credits his religious faith for giving him strength and providing many of the solutions he was seeking.

Some people in his position are driven by the lure of wealth and money. In Griff's case, it is the desire to be part of a creative process and to experience start-to-finish responsibility.

As a pharmacist, he dispensed a prescription but never saw the outcome with the patient. As a pilot in the military, he brought fuel to other aircraft and then moved on. But as a real estate developer, he could negotiate a creatively financed business deal, then see it through to a finished product, with grass growing and kids playing. His commitment is such that he tells his children and employees that if they don't really enjoy the business and really enjoy coming to work, then they need to be doing something else.

To control his attitude, Griff relies on his wife and several trusted friends for guidance. He acknowledges that there are many factors outside of his control, like interest rates and government policies, but he works hard at anticipating external factors and controlling what he can. When the market changes, he and his firm roll with the punches and adapt to the opportunities of the day.

Other than changing his career from pharmacist to real estate developer, Griff has never experienced the LOOKING phase in his career. In his case, it was a calculated career decision to change. He assessed all of his opportunities and deliberately chose to dismount from his position at the pharmacy by letting his license lapse. He simply did not want to go back that way, so he burned the bridge in order to assure his success in the new endeavor.

Today, he keeps raising the bar to maintain excitement. He loves to teach people the business and help them compress the learning curve. And he offers this advice to all of us: Whether we're facing big problems like impending bankruptcy or the smaller problems we all face every day, don't duck your problems or put them on the back burner. Face them head on. Go talk to the people you're dealing with . You'd be surprised sometimes what they're willing to do. And if you're really working with a problem-solving attitude, they're likely to say, "He's better at getting out of these things than we are — why don't we work with him?"

SAM COLEMAN

Sam Coleman is another Super Achiever, and for many years, he has been a master at following the positive attitude cycle in his life, despite a rather unpleasant childhood.

When he was 8, his father took off, leaving Sam and his mother in a small country town without support. His mother married again, this time to an alcoholic, and a mean one, at that. After several years, she divorced and married yet another alcoholic. With the family income paying for alcohol, there wasn't much money for anything else. So Sam was raised in sheer poverty.

A lot of people with a childhood like that would probably be bitter, and might even use their upbringing as an excuse for a lack of success in their lives. Sam Coleman isn't bitter.

In fact, he considers himself lucky that his father left when he did because he was too young to fall prey to the lure of alcohol himself. And being poor gave Sam something else — the burning desire to become wealthy.

His first job was in an auto parts store, and by the time he was 26, he had saved up enough money to go into the parts business. The business just wasn't very successful, and when the lease came due, he simply closed it down. A year or so later, he got excited about the auto parts business again and opened another one. Within two years, he got tired of the long hours and the seven-day weeks, and this frustration caused him to go LOOKING for other opportunities.

He sold his parts business for a very small sum and bought a franchise from Success Motivation Institute, a company which sold motivational cassette tapes. For four years, he listened to the inspiring words of authors including Napoleon Hill, Norman Vincent Peale and W. Clement Stone as he went about selling SMI's products. Today, he credits this period of his life as a turning point because it taught him to have faith and confidence in himself and caused him to fill his mind with positive, uplifting thoughts on a daily basis.

After four years with SMI, Sam sold his franchise to pursue a business partnership in Tampa. Things didn't work out, and even though he managed to avoid bankruptcy, Sam was broke once again. He moved to Albuquerque to start over and started three businesses: a burglar alarm company, a wholesale candy company and a jewelry business. The jewelry business turned out to be a real success, so he closed down the burglar alarm business and sold the candy business to devote all of his time to selling jewelry.

Perhaps because it was financially successful and was allowing Sam to achieve his desire to be wealthy that he has managed to remain committed to the jewelry business to this day despite the inevitable frustration he experienced. Each time frustration would strike, he said he got "sort of angry — not at anyone or anything in particular — just angry." This anger caused him to "come out of the corner and make things happen." A lot of times, he simply had to have his back up against the wall before he would really come out swinging.

Approximately seven years into the business, Sam nearly went broke again when he moved his factory to South Dakota. Once more, however, he rose above the frustration of this experience by working harder and longer hours. He recommitted to the business and did whatever it took to make the sales and get the working capital from the banks. Once, he even had to go all the way to Chicago for the operating funds to keep his business going. But he never blamed anybody for his troubles — he said he never thought about blaming anyone else.

Sam said he never thought about recommitting to his goal, either. It just happened. He said he did his best when his back was against the wall, that he would grit his teeth and get it done. But he also said he could see his dream failing. "I could just see my dream slipping away of having a big, successful business." In Sam's case, his motivation might just be fear of failure because twice a year, he experiences a dream about going to work in some menial job. He said he wakes up depressed when that happens.

Able to retire at the age of 53, Sam now likes to work on his golf game. When he first started playing, he wasn't very good. He wanted to be shooting in the 70s, and he was experiencing frustration with his performance. He saw himself failing. But instead of taking up another sport, or blaming his troubles on something else, Sam put the positive attitude cycle to work. He revisited his dream about becoming a better golfer, then took positive action by setting the goal to improve. He sought out a mentor for golf lessons. Several years later, he still practices, reads books on the subject and takes lessons to improve.

About attitude, Sam said this: "Your attitude is your personality on display. It's a group of thoughts that you habitually think, so in order to change your attitude, you go back down to the core of it and change your habits of thinking. If you change enough of those habits in a positive way, then your attitude will change. And it's a permanent change — it's not just like I have a good attitude today. If you change enough of them, and they are habits, by golly, it'll change you the rest of your life."

GERRY LANE

Gerry Lane is a Super Achiever who has made his living by selling cars — lots of them. Starting from scratch nearly 45 years ago, he grew Gerry Lane Enterprises into its present form — an organization consisting of nine corporations, 25 franchises and more than 300 employees. Last year, Gerry Lane Enterprises, based in Baton Rouge, Louisiana, sold more than $130 million worth of cars, accessories and service.

Born poor and raised on a cattle ranch and farm, Gerry grew up in the country. There were no telephones or televisions where he lived, and the nearest school was 5 miles away. He was hyperactive as a child and remembers being tied to a chair for restraint. He learned to compensate for these difficulties by reading books. He read books while riding on the school bus, sitting in study halls, even at recess. He read so much that he got a certificate of recognition for checking out every book in the school's library. He still reads every day — books on history and books with positive, inspirational material.

158

Despite his love of books, Gerry did not graduate from college. Instead, he earned a degree from the School of Hard Knocks, which he claims is the best university if you can afford the tuition. Every time he makes a mistake, he smiles and says, "There's another $5,000 toward my doctorate."

In the same way that he dedicated himself to reading, Gerry brings a tremendous commitment to his work. More than 40 years after starting to work in the automobile business, he is still "fired up" about going to work each day. He doesn't want to retire.

Gerry attributes this lifelong commitment to two things. First and foremost was his desire to become a pillar of the community. As a young man, he looked around and noticed that car dealers were respected, contributing members of society. He decided to emulate these successful dealers and become one himself.

Starting out as a mechanic at age 21, it was only a short time before he was promoted into management. He was convinced that "because [he] had a positive attitude, management offers would come [his] way." And they did. He became a service manager and then a new car sales manager for two different dealerships before becoming a general sales manager.

Gerry had written down some realistic goals for himself. His dream was to become a dealer by the time he was 50. That meant he needed to be a general sales manager at 45 and a sales manager at 40. Not surprisingly, the young man with these realistic goals achieved them all. What is surprising is that he achieved them all so early.

He was a new car sales manager by 26 and a general sales manager by 28. At the tender age of 35, he had saved enough money to buy a dealership. Less than two years later, he bought a second dealership. At 38, he bought three more.

Today, he owns 25 franchises.

The second driving force behind Gerry's incredible commitment was his desire to become rich. Perhaps the poverty of his youth made him fear being poor, or perhaps it was the youthful dedication he demonstrated by reading all of those books. Either way, he was able to fix in his mind a singular purpose and stick with it until it was realized.

In the beginning, he was not particularly excited about the car business. "I didn't fall in love with the car business," he recalled. "I was looking for a job."

But somewhere along the line, his goal-setting, dedicated effort and his desire to overcome poverty combined to bring about a perpetual EXCITEMENT phase in Gerry. To recycle continuously through the EXCITEMENT phase for more than 40 years is a tremendous feat. Even though he often battles frustration, he says he avoids the LOOKING phase by staying committed to his goals and reading positive material every day. Unconsciously, he also applies all of the other methods for RECOMMITMENT described in Chapter 7 of this book.

He once thought about leaving the car business and going into real estate. Instead, he began redreaming the dream.

"I just sat down and went back to the basics," he said. "I went back and thought about what I had been doing when I started selling cars and how I was so enthused about the cars. I had never owned a new car. I wanted everybody to be as enthused about it as I was.

"I also looked at the automotive transportation business. I could see where cars and trucks were something that were going to wear out and have to be replaced. I could see where land was something you would sell one time. Dirt doesn't wear out, and dirt doesn't have to be replaced."

Another frustrating time occurred while he was working

for a dealership in California. The dealer's philosophy was to sell a car, then turn around and find someone else to sell. They did not believe in service or in repeat business. This attitude was frustrating to Gerry, and he considered leaving the car business.

This time, he recommitted by deciding to be the best he could be, by taking a bad situation and making a good situation out of it. In other words, he set some short-term goals and took immediate action. He began by taking a Dale Carnegie sales course. He continued with several specialized courses at UCLA. One course in particular shows how dedicated he really was — a sales psychology course that was taught at two in the morning. His fellow salesmen laughed at him, but Gerry ignored the ridicule and prepared himself for the future. He knew that when opportunity comes to knock on your door, you've got to be dressed and ready to leave.

At other frustrating times, Gerry consulted his mentors for guidance. The list includes Herb Polk, who was one of Gerry's first bosses, a variety of successful authors and business people, Dale Carnegie Training and the Chevrolet factory. He faithfully took their advice and put it to work. "They are all successful, with tried and true methods," he said. "All I need to do is what they tell me to do. Five percent of what they suggest might fail and even cost me some money, but the other 95 percent will make me rich."

To Gerry, everyone is his superior in some way, and he goes out of his way to learn from others. He said his businesses are constantly looking for people who would be a positive addition to the business. He believes that attitude and enthusiasm are the keys to success.

"Everybody's gifted," he said. "Everybody can do the job, but the person with enthusiasm, who wants to do it, has got the job done. One person can make a difference. Enthusiasm is the difference."

At the same time, he warns that negative people are not going to be promoted, and negative people are not going to be business owners. While management is always looking for people with positive attitudes, they simply will not hire people with negative attitudes. He says he has never seen a negative person who got ahead.

Many car dealers (and other business owners, too) are quick to blame the economy when their business isn't doing well. They will tell you that they make money only in the good times and have to suffer through the bad ones. Gerry believes in making a profit regardless of the economy, and in all of his years in the car business, he has never run in the red. He is a shining example of an executive who takes responsibility for results instead of passing the buck by blaming external events and forces.

When a business is doing poorly, it is almost always the fault of management. Gerry understands this well. He has built his incredible business by finding and acquiring businesses whose owners were in the LOOKING phase — owners who became FRUSTRATED and lost the ability to RECOMMIT. Unable to restore EXCITEMENT, they failed to produce desirable results.

To avoid failure in your business, learn from Gerry Lane, and keep your business in the EXCITEMENT phase!

TOM FRANK

Tom Frank is chief executive officer and chairman of the board for Conn Appliance Inc. Conn's is a major dealer of appliances and home entertainment products, with 35 stores throughout Louisiana and Texas. The company, based in Beaumont, Texas, employs more than 850 people. Last year, revenue from its rental, service and credit operations was more than $190 million.

Like Gerry Lane, Tom Frank did not start out with a burning passion for what has become his life's work. When C. W. Conn Jr. offered him the opportunity to start a service department for the family's appliance business, Tom was already working in his chosen profession as a woodworking teacher. Tom accepted the new job primarily because of its economic benefits, but he also brought with him a commitment born of a strong work ethic and excitement for the opportunity to build a service organization.

After he had proven his capabilities with the service end of the business, Tom was given other projects. When a particular aspect of the business needed correction or growth, the assignment was given to Tom. These assignments played a major role in his commitment to Conn's because they gave him a sense of autonomy. For the most part, he was able to make his own decisions and see projects through to an end result.

Additionally, the atmosphere at Conn's was conducive for success. His employer was not only caring and sensitive enough to mentor him over rough spots, but he was also fair in compensation for results achieved. Many of these projects resulted in promotions, so each opportunity offered another EXCITEMENT phase and another opportunity to RECOMMIT to the business. Today, more than 30 years later, Tom is still excited about the business and more committed than ever.

Were there any frustrations in this utopian environment? Of course. They fell mainly in the area of human relations. As the youngest among his peers, Tom found himself unable to follow through on some decisions because of conflicts. He insists that some of his problems with others had tangible causes but readily admits that some were perceived, as well.

Early in his career, he tended to blame others for these problems.

Later in his career, with frustrations at a boiling point, he began LOOKING at a career with a major electronics firm. He checked the other company out thoroughly and was about to leave. He changed his mind at the last minute because of a recommitment talk with his boss, C. W. Conn Jr. The elder man gently counseled Tom that while he would probably be successful at the new job, he could be even more successful by staying where he was. Tom decided to take that advice and is glad he did.

For much of his career, Tom continued to blame others when he experienced frustration — not all of the time, mind you, but in many important matters. Somewhere along the line, he finally made the split-second choice to take personal responsibility for any problems he was facing. This is when he really started growing.

Today, he modifies his own behavior instead of reacting to the behavior of others. "I was always trying to control their behavior, and change them, instead of focusing on what I had the ability to change," he said. Now, he counsels others, including his own son, to make the same split-second choice. He also said that he would have probably been where he is today a lot earlier in his career if he had accepted this principle from the start.

He also believes in the productive use of controlled anger. "Anger really has very little use, but I've found it has some usefulness if it is controlled and well thought out and you understand that you are using that as a technique as opposed to a reaction," Tom said. "I think that's the difference in how you handle anger. I think there are appropriate times to be angry. I think you should be angry if your company is not doing well. I think you should be angry when a customer is abused or not taken care of.

"On the other hand, if anger replaces positive direction and planning, or if it's overused, then it's harmful."

For recommitment, Tom relies on a variety of methods. When things get frustrating, he tries assessing the situation, dreaming about possible solutions, changing or adjusting goals and sometimes taking a vacation. He also consults a lot of mentors, including management consultants and training companies. His red-flag partners include his younger brother and four or five industry contacts.

As you might expect, Tom spends a lot of time on organization-wide issues. Two years ago, when Tom took over as chairman, his company was only half as prosperous as it is today. As the transition to new leadership began, there was a lot of apprehension, anxiety and fear. In other words, the organization as a whole was thrown quickly into a state of FRUSTRATION. Tom sensed this. Through his leadership, he was able to get the organization to dream the dream again and to recommit.

After setting short-term goals, the company began working to achieve them. EXCITEMENT displaced FRUSTRATION, and the organization prospered. In less than two years, the company grew from $100 million in sales to nearly $200 million, and increased profits, as well. That growth is now creating problems of its own, as well as new FRUSTRATION, but Tom is already working on RECOMMITMENT strategies.

All organizations are subject to this pattern. They cycle through EXCITEMENT, FRUSTRATION and RECOMMITMENT in the same manner individuals do. Most of the time, leaders in organizations are continuously communicating the company vision, setting new goals and seeking advice in order to stay within the positive cycle. Occasionally, an organization will be unable to RECOMMIT. When this happens, it will begin LOOKING for new leadership. If it doesn't seek and find new leadership in time, it may fail.

Tom Frank understands this well. He understands that his job as leader is to keep the organization in an EXCITEMENT phase. Like a good supervisor would do, he continuously monitors the organization and its customers for signs of FRUSTRATION. He does this by randomly visiting stores and riding on delivery trucks. When he finds evidence of FRUSTRATION, he takes action to help eliminate it. Sometimes, this requires problem-solving, and sometimes it takes corporate RECOMMITMENT.

If you were to visit Conn's, you might be privileged to see the supersophisticated method uses to solve problems — chalkboards. There are chalkboards all over the place, and if you walk around, you will see groups of employees focused on solving problems with these chalkboards. Conn's gets several benefits from this method.

First, problems are identified and solved. Second, they benefit from the insights of a number of people. And finally, their people have immediate ownership of the solution, so they are much more likely to make it work. This, in turn, relieves management of the need to sell a solution to those who have to implement it.

For corporate RECOMMITMENT, Tom uses many of the same methods he uses personally. He knows from experience that individuals in key positions are often the key to the corporate attitude and has observed that their FRUSTRATION phase occurs earlier than that of the organization as a whole. He picks up on the anxiety and the shortness of tempers when people are asked to make changes.

To turn this around, he leads the leaders through RECOMMITMENT.

"The key people in the key slots are really the organization as a whole, and they influence the other people around them," he said. "It just has sort of a ripple effect all the way out."

To keep the organization on track, Tom also works with individuals on a personal level. Remembering his own experience with C. W. Conn Jr., he stresses that calm, sensitive counseling of employees is essential. His goal is to help them see and consider alternative behaviors that might be more productive than the ones they were contemplating. Many times, he said, the more productive people in the organization are the ones who have the most difficult issues to sort through.

In an overall sense, Tom believes an organization's culture has a lot to do with its attitude. At Conn's, a lot of the culture came from its founder. On one occasion early in Tom's career, Tom and the founder's son discussed financial statements with him. His response was, "I really don't care what these statements say. You and C.W. just got together with the accountant, and he published it the way you all wanted him to, anyway." Then he added, "I want to know about three things: I want to know how much inventory is in the barn. Is it all there? How much money is in the bank? And are all the bills paid?"

It was a simplistic approach that cut right to the heart of problems.

On another occasion, they brought up a customer satisfaction survey for discussion. Tom and the younger Conn were showing the founder the numbers and how 95 percent of the customers were happy when he said, "You know, I really don't care about the 95 percent that are happy. I want to know about the 5 percent that are unhappy. I'd like to know their names and then, by the way, I want you to make them happy before you go home tonight." This commitment to customers is just one of the reasons that customers are committed to Conn's.

Tom Frank is a Super-Achieving executive because he leads others to impressive results. Conn's is a Super-Achieving company because leadership at the top keeps things simple, focuses on what is really important and makes sure all of the stakeholders are committed and excited. Simply stated, they spend all of the time they can in the EXCITEMENT phase, and it pays big dividends for customers, employees, vendors and owners.

MIKE FRANCIS

Mike Francis and his wife Diana like to play in the mud — a special kind of mud known as drilling mud. As co-owners of Francis Drilling Fluids, they have been busy supplying products and services to the oil and gas industry since 1977. Their company, based in Crowley, Louisiana, employs 150 people and sales revenue exceeds $20 million.

As a young man of 17, Mike went to work in the oil fields of South Louisiana. After holding a variety of jobs, he decided to specialize in drilling fluids.

Drilling fluids are very important components in an oil well venture. When a company begins drilling for oil, it is creating a pipeline several miles deep into the earth. Various drilling fluids help wash the cuttings up to the surface, while drilling mud strengthens the walls surrounding the pipeline. Geological structures vary, and pressures within the earth can pose unique hazards. A mud company like Francis Drilling Fluids has to deal with these variables, often on an emergency basis.

A few years into his career, Mike was working as a self-employed drilling fluids engineer when he noticed a need for better service in that area of the oil and gas industry. He and his wife had been putting money aside to buy furniture for a house they were building. Instead of buying the furniture, they leased an 18 wheeler, and invested in a rundown drilling fluids facility. Eight weeks later, Mike had driven 8000 miles and lost 15 pounds.

Largely due to Mike and Diana's dedication to excellent service, their business grew quickly, and earned respect in the industry.

Personally, I believe that building a $20 million company from scratch in less than 20 years is enough to qualify a man as a Super Achiever, but Mike Francis has done more than that. For the last four years he has been working in the political arena as well. Currently serving as the Chairman of the Republican Party in Louisiana, he has been actively trying to make the world a better place. Many people give him credit for historic progress.

When I think about Mike, a number of positive characteristics come to mind. He is down to earth, and a warm leader with compassion for others. Because he can see things through other people's eyes, he is a visionary who sees potential even in adversity. Burning inside him is the flame of enthusiasm for what he believes in. He maintains an open, trusting relationship with everyone in his company, and while he has high expectations for their performance, he holds himself accountable for high levels of productivity as well. Able to generate excitement in himself and others, he asks others only what he asks of himself.

Listen to him talk, and you will think he has never experienced a frustrating time in his life. Dig a little deeper, and he will admit that, yes, there have been some difficult moments. Probe even further and you will uncover the secrets that have helped him become a Super Achiever.

What are those secrets? Not surprisingly, we've been talking about them throughout this book.

Instead of looking for an easy way out, he accepts responsibility and looks for opportunities to advance. He believes in staying excited and enthusiastic.

He knows frustration and anger are just part of life, so he is prepared for them. He also knows frustration is not the mood in which to accomplish goals. When frustration shows up — he acknowledges it, goes through it, expresses it, gets a grip on it, and gets over it.

He keeps the reward out front, faces the problem, and takes action.

With respect to others, he observes that human nature tends to make us all somewhat negative. Leaders need to understand this and overcome it with what they say and do every day.

As a young entrepreneur, Mike and his wife faced the same kinds of problems that most entrepreneurs face — insufficient funding, employee shortages, strong competition, uncertain prices, and a negative world. Early on, one of their biggest problems was trying to borrow the funds they needed for additional people, equipment, and facilities. Mike remembers going into several banks with excitement and dreams in his heart, only to find bankers that were neither excited nor enthusiastic about his plans. Mike was SHOCKED at their reaction. In spite of the FRUSTRATION, he moved quickly through DENIAL, FEAR, and ANGER to RECOMMITMENT, where he put together a variety of creative banking solutions. This positive, solution-oriented approach has helped Francis Drilling Fluids to prosper.

About four years ago, Mike and some friends were discussing politics. The conversation focused mainly on all the problems they saw with government. He realized that griping and blaming others would not get the results he wanted.

Again, he decided to take action on his own and make some positive things happen. This was the split second choice that led to the Louisiana Republican Party Chairmanship.

He realizes that organizations experience frustration, too. This is one reason he watches carefully for signs of commitment and enthusiasm in new employees. He believes that life at home affects life at work, and tries to help his employees keep their entire lives in an EXCITEMENT phase.

Mike expects his employees to handle frustration on their own whenever possible, but he also teaches them what a pair of boy scouts once learned about walking on railroad tracks. One scout, walking alone on a rail, kept losing his balance. The other scout, seeing this, took a position on the opposite rail, and suggested they hold hands to keep each other from falling. Trust and support like that make an organization strong.

From experience, Mike knows that employee commitment and enthusiasm are key attributes in his employees. This basic truth allowed him to survive a few years ago when his entire management team left to start a business of their own. Their primary strategy was aggressive pursuit of the most profitable aspect of the drilling fluids business. This would be a tough and frustration time for any business, but Francis Drilling Fluids is the type of organization that makes positive things happen. This time it was the organization that fought through the shock, denial, fear and anger before recommitting to the goals of the business.

Mike believes that his people are his greatest asset. He says several of them worked day and night to keep the business open during the crisis.

Like many Super Achievers, Mike credits his success to faith in God. At a worship service one Sunday, Mike's preacher gave everyone in the congregation a plastic fork.

Mike says that reminds him of life's many small turning points, and how each of those opportunities has life changing potential.

Mike Francis makes the unconscious shift to the silver cloud because he knows there will be mountain tops alongside the valleys. He stays focused on remaining excited and enthusiastic — no matter what the odds. You can, too!

CLOSING COMMENT

Like love and hate, success and failure are very closely related. Golfers win by one stroke. Football teams win by one point. Horses win by a nose. Competitive runners and swimmers win by microseconds.

Winners may only be inches ahead of their competition or their own past performance, but *they consistently look forward and move forward.* That's what makes them a success. In our own case, we may only need to be a tiny bit better than we already are to win.

As these examples have shown, to be truly productive, we need to be in an EXCITEMENT phase. We stay there by replacing our negative thoughts and feelings with positive action towards our dreams and goals.

The key to overcoming any fear we face is to maintain the original commitment clearly in front of us where it can help pull us forward. Since repeated negative cycles only serve to reduce our commitment with the downward spiral they produce, it is critical to repeat the positive cycle and strengthen our resolve instead.

Success is almost assured if we remain committed to our dreams, and we become Super Achievers when we learn to recommit on a regular basis over a long haul.

Chapter 14

The Race: Get Up
When You Fall

"Our greatest glory is not in never falling, but in rising every time we fall."

From the Chinese

"Fall seven times, stand up eight."

From the Japanese

"It's not how many times you get bucked off; it's how many times you get back on."

From the American Rodeo

"Perseverance is not a long race; it is many short races one after another."

Walter Elliott

THE RACE
(D. H. Groberg)

"QUIT! GIVE UP! YOU'RE BEATEN!" They shout out and plead,
There's just too much against you now, this time you can't succeed.
And as I start to hang my head in front of failure's face,
My downward fall is broken by the memory of a race.

And hope refills my weakened will as I recall that scene.
For just the thought of that short race rejuvenates my being.
A children's race, young boys, young men; now I remember well.
Excitement, sure, but also fear; it wasn't hard to tell.

They all lined up so full of hope. Each thought to win that race
Or tie for first, or if not that, at least take second place.
And fathers watched from off the side, each cheering for his son.
And each boy hoped to show his dad that he would be the one.

The whistle blew and off they went, young hearts and hopes of fire.
To win, to be the hero there, was each young boy's desire.
And one boy in particular, his dad was in the crowd,
Was running near the lead and thought, "My Dad will be so proud."

But as he speeded down the field across a shallow dip,
The little boy who thought to win, lost his step and slipped.
Trying hard to catch himself, his hands flew out to brace,
And mid the laughter of the crowd, he fell flat on his face.

So down he fell and with him hope. He couldn't win it now.
Embarrassed, sad, he only wished to disappear somehow.
But as he fell, his dad stood up and showed his anxious face.
Which to the boy so clearly said, "Get up and win that race!"

The Race: Get Up When You Fall

He quickly rose, no damage done — behind a bit, that's all,
And ran with all his mind and might to make up for his fall.
So anxious to restore himself to catch up and to win,
His mind went faster than his legs. He slipped and fell again.

He wished that he had quit before with only one disgrace.
I'm hopeless as a runner now, I shouldn't try to race.
But, in a laughing crowd he searched and found his father's face
That steady look that said again, "Get up and win the race."

So, he jumped up to try again. Ten yards behind the last.
If I'm to gain those yards, he thought, I've got to run real fast.
Exceeding everything he had, he regained eight or ten,
But trying so hard to catch the lead, he slipped and fell again.

Defeat! He lay there silently, a tear dropped from his eye.
There's no sense running anymore -- three strikes I'm out -- why try?
The will to rise had disappeared, all hope had fled away.
So far behind, so error prone, closer all the way.

I've lost, so what's the use, he thought, I'll live with my disgrace.
But then he thought about his dad, who soon he'd have to face.
"Get up," an echo sounded low. "Get up and take your place.
"You were not meant for failure here, get up and win the race."

With borrowed will, "Get up," it said, "You haven't lost at all."
"For winning is not more than this: to rise each time you fall."
So up he rose to win once more. And with a new commit,
He resolved that win or lose, at least he wouldn't quit.

SPLIT SECOND CHOICE

So far behind the others now, the most he'd ever been.
Still he gave it all he had and ran as though to win.
Three times he'd fallen stumbling, three times he'd rose again.
Too far behind to hope to win, he still ran to the end.

They cheered the winning runner as he crossed first place.
Head high and proud and happy; no falling, no disgrace.
But when the fallen youngster crossed the line, last place,
The crowd gave him the greater cheer for finishing the race.

And even though he came in last, with head bowed low, unproud;
You would have thought he won the race, to listen to the crowd.
And to his Dad he sadly said, "I didn't do so well."
"To me you won," his father said, "You rose each time you fell."

And when things seem dark and hard and difficult to face,
The memory of that little boy helps me in my race.
For all of life is like that race, with ups and downs and all,
And all you have to do to win is rise each time you fall.
"QUIT! GIVE UP! YOU'RE BEATEN!" they still shout in my face.
But another voice within me says, "GET UP AND WIN THE RACE!"

    May God bless you and your family's future as you take responsibility for your attitude.

Jim Winner

("The Race" used by permission from author, D.H. Groberg)

Epilogue

Near the end of the movie version of **Jonathan Livingston Seagull**, adapted from Richard Bach's magnificent book, Jonathan has a conversation with his student, Fletcher Lynd Seagull:

Jonathan Livingston Seagull:
   "It is time to return to the flock."
Fletcher Lynd Seagull:
   "Why?"
Jonathan Livingston Seagull:
   "You have a gift to give...
After pausing, Jonathan continues:
   "Vicious. Clumsy. A seagull hardly knows how to walk. But don't you see, Fletcher? A seagull wasn't made to walk. He was made to fly. And when he learns to fly, he's the purest, loveliest, most graceful creature alive. True for you. True for me. True for all the flock. We can soar free across the sky. But how often we don't want to. That's the gift we can give. To help those who want to learn find what they love to do."

This book was written for you — so that you, too, can fly above the clouds with a positive, productive attitude.

APPENDIX
SAMPLE COMMITMENT FORM

What am I committing to do as I begin this career (project, relationship, marriage)? What is my commitment?

_____

_____

_____

Why am I committed to this career (project, relationship, marriage)? What am I excited about? Who else is excited and why? What are my motives and reasons for undertaking this commitment?

_____

_____

_____

I would describe my dream of the future in the following way (include sights, sounds, smells, feelings):

_____

_____

_____

Fulfillment of this commitment will provide me with the following reward(s):

_____

_____

_____

If you would like information on multiple book discounts, or if you are interested in scheduling James L. Winner for a seminar or workshop, please call or write:

The Winner Institute
2251 Drusilla Lane, Suite C
Baton Rouge, LA 70806
800-256-9222

☐ Yes, please send me _____ additional copies of
SPLIT SECOND CHOICE
$17.95 + $3.00 Tax, Shipping and Handling
Per Copy

QUANTITY DISCOUNTS
10 to 19 copies --- 5%

20 to 49 copies --- 10%

50 to 99 copies --- 15%

100 copies or more --- 20%

Please include an additional 10% for shipping & handling

Enclosed is:

☐ Company P.O.   ☐ Check   ☐ Visa/MC # _____ exp. _____

Name _____ Title _____

Signature _____

Company _____

Address _____

City _____ State _____ Zip _____

Telephone _____ Fax _____

The Winners
2251 Drusilla Lane, Suite C   Baton Rouge, LA 70806
Tel. (800) 256-9222   Fax (504) 925-5121

NOTES